PRAISE

Vertalino's approach is nothing short of revolutionary! By encouraging women to love themselves first and set boundaries, *The Ladies Playbook* empowers women to raise their standards and get the love they deserve.

Alinka Rutkowska | USA Today and Wall Street Journal Bestselling Author

Melanie Joy Vertalino's *The Ladies Playbook* shakes up how women approach dating. It's an empowering reminder to embrace your self-worth, take charge of your love life, and never settle for less than you deserve.

Jeanette Leeds | Founder, Leeds & Co

In this book, Melanie teaches women how to take ownership of their personal and professional lives. This is an essential read for women who wants to build high-value relationships based on mutual respect, confidence, and self-love.

Dr. Michelle Wicmandy | Global Marketing Campaigns Manager, KBC Adjunct Professor of Marketing, University of Houston-Downtown

THE LADIES PLAYBOOK

How to Get Your Way with A Man

By Melanie Joy Vertalino

ISBN **979-8-3306-2468-3** (pbk)
ISBN **979-8-34412-557-2** (hcv)

Library of Congress Control Number: **2024923059**

Unlock Your Power!

DOWNLOAD YOUR FREE GUIDE

ThePlaybookForLadies.com

Learn Ten Tips
to Magnetize Men

TABLE OF CONTENTS

I dedicate this book to my father,
James Joseph Vertalino,
who has always been there for me.
I LOVE YOU ALWAYS!

"To realize your potential, you must
look beyond the end of yourself,
realizing that where you end, is most
likely where you actually begin."

Craig D. Lounsbrough

INTRODUCTION

Recently, I was discussing this book with my dearest friend and went on to tell her that it is literally my "baby" and is incredibly important to me. It's a culmination of a lifetime of difficult experiences I've endured and come out on the other side of. It's so important to me that this book gets into the hands of as many women as possible because I don't want anyone else to go through what I went through in my life with men. While discussing this with her, I began to cry because of how important this is. I don't want you to have to struggle or suffer in order to be loved anymore! And you don't have to!

I started this book more than seven years ago, and since then, the title has changed repeatedly—as have I. Something always felt like it was missing or incomplete. The fact is, I was the one who was incomplete. Everything I do needs to feel authentic. Staying true to myself and my intuition are values at the core of my being. *The Ladies Playbook: How to Get Your Way with a Man* is about implementing real change and growth at an internal soul level and its permanent change. It's not about game playing or manipulation. I want you to love yourself and have the best life you possibly can.

I'm going to talk to you like I would to my best friend. She would tell you that I say what needs to be said. Sometimes, we really do need someone who cares about us to get in our face and tell us exactly what we need to hear to grow and change. Notice I said "someone who cares about us" because, otherwise, it just feels like we're being attacked. Please know that I am coming from a place of understanding and love, because I have been there repeatedly.

Please note that we are all at different levels of development. Some of the information in this book may be exactly what you need to hear in the moment, and some you may temporarily brush off because it may not currently "click" or apply to you at this time. Try and keep those pieces of information in the back of your mind. Try to "put pins in them," which will light up in the future when you face the experience or a similar experience again. You may need it one day. If there's anything you don't understand, go back and reread it, because each chapter builds upon the previous one. I recommend reading this book more than once because I have so much life-changing information in it.

I will teach you how to become a high-quality woman who will attract a high-quality man. You will value yourself more and finally start making yourself a priority. This is for women who have been unlucky in love and want to know how to turn that around and, finally, have the love of their dreams! We live in a mirror universe where you need to become what it is that you want in order to attract it to you!

WHO IS THIS BOOK FOR?

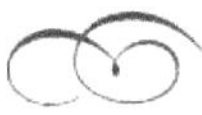

- Women who have not had the best of luck with men
- If you've been chasing men, been deceived by men, manipulated, or generally mistreated
- If you've spent most of your life in your masculine energy taking care of men
- If you're a people pleaser or don't know how to tell people no
- If you tend to attract narcissists, sociopaths, psychopaths, or any other type of toxic men
- If you've found yourself in a "pattern" where you keep repeating the same experiences with different men
- If you've fallen victim to unrequited love or "limerence"
- If you're sick and tired of being alone but can't stand the thought of having another partner who doesn't prioritize you
- If you keep getting ghosted by men and don't know why
- If you've never made yourself a priority before or put your OWN needs first
- If you've spent so much time caring for others and now don't even know what you want out of life
- If you feel shame, guilt, or any unworthiness
- If you've had a rough childhood, rough adolescence, or a totally rough life in general
- If you want to start being treated like the Goddess you are
- If you're ready to lean back into your feminine receiving energy
- If you're ready to take charge of your life and stop dating little boys and Peter Pans
- If you're ready to become a HIGH-VAUE WOMAN, this is your book!

With so much love,
Melanie

"Self-transformation commences with a period of self-questioning. Questions lead to more questions, bewilderment leads to new discoveries, and growing personal awareness leads to transformation in how a person lives. Purposeful modification of the self only commences with revising our mind's internal functions. Revamped internal functions eventually alter how we view our external environment."

— Kilroy J. Oldster, Dead Toad Scrolls

CHAPTER 1
GET REAL WITH YOURSELF

"Human beings are not born once and for all on the day their mothers give birth to them, but ... life obliges them over and over again to give birth to themselves."
~ Gabriel García Márquez

Get real with yourself. Whether you accept yourself or repress yourself, you know yourself. Being real is about being honest. Without honesty, there is nothing. Are you prepared to take a good look at yourself and be brutally honest with what you see? As they say, the comfort zone is a beautiful place, but nothing ever grows there. Change is difficult but necessary on our journey of self-improvement. All the fun is in the journey anyways!

The first step to getting real with yourself is to accept yourself right now—every single part: your personality, your body, your face, your life, your history, and your choices. One of my favorite authors, RJ Spina, who healed himself from chest-down paralysis in 2016, always says, "You must learn to accept and love yourself, warts and all," meaning, you must accept and love every single part of you. This includes your jiggly thighs, any wrinkles, or cellulite you may have. If you don't accept who you are, the entire foundation of your being is a lie. Nothing can be built upon a lie because it isn't real. You came here with a specific purpose that only you know. Because you exist, you have value. And that is all you need. The models in magazines are a lie. Everything on social media is also a lie. Don't be a lie. Every single one of us is flawed; it's part of the grand design. All you can do is accept, forgive, and love yourself. Always be true to yourself. Ask yourself, "What do I want?"

*"There is a very fine line between helping
another and hurting yourself."*
~ Jacob Rappleye

Learn to set your own boundaries so that nobody can push you past them. Learn to be strong in your own skin and you will never need to go out of your way to get anyone to like you. It's not about being liked; it's about being respected. People are flighty and change their minds daily. Never do anything for the opinion of another. Work to please yourself, not others. The most attractive quality in a person is self-respect. People who respect themselves are respected by others as well. Never look to others to tell you about yourself. Know yourself, by yourself.

Don't compare yourself to others because nobody else should be YOUR standard. *Make sure you grasp that before you move on.* That is the beginning of the path to creating an inner glow within yourself that becomes seductive to everyone you meet. It's not about what you look like, or what you weigh, or how much money you have. Superficial technicalities are always just temporary. If you could learn to glow from the inside right now and for always, I could tell you to just stop reading.

One thing you need to do is confront your unseen self, the parts of you that you have been avoiding, are unaware of, or choose not to see. Some call this our "shadow," which is an aspect of our inner child. Each time we repress ourselves by not being authentic, we're fragmenting ourselves. Over time, if left unintegrated, the shadow grows by fragmenting each time we conceal our truth. This is where our "triggers" come from when we become irritated. If you're a person who reacts, rather than responds, you're likely operating from your shadow or your unconscious. It's like being on autopilot for years and not even knowing it! It's these parts of you that need to be examined, evaluated, and integrated into your being. You need to have the courage to step outside of yourself and look at yourself through the eyes of love. If you do it with your own eyes, you will only see what you have always seen before. You need to look with new eyes. Try journaling from the perspective of a close friend or a mentor and imagine how they would view you.

You can start entertaining other people's perspectives. See through their eyes. When you can see a situation through the eyes of another, then you can begin to do the same with yourself. This is the beginning of true change and a priceless tool that will keep you constantly moving forward and advancing in all of life's endeavors. Seeing yourself and life through multiple perspectives is a wonderful way to learn to understand yourself and the world around you.

If you are still judging yourself, you will have an extremely hard time with this. It's in our nature to be defensive when we feel we're being attacked or criticized. We all want to be loved and accepted. I want you to think about where the advice or suggestions come from. Is it coming from someone who genuinely cares about you and wants to see you excel? Always consider the source. Your gut or intuition knows all the answers if you ask it. See how it feels. See if the criticism truly is constructive from someone who cares. Once you can determine a person's motives, they can no longer be a threat to your peace of mind. Always use your own discernment when taking opinions from others. Judging yourself is detrimental to your health. Give yourself the same breaks and compassion that you would give a close friend. Please forgive yourself and others for the past. You were always doing the best you could with the information you had.

If you have come to accept, forgive, and fully love yourself, confronting your unseen self will not be as challenging as you believe. I know that you love yourself, too. You know how I know? You wouldn't have purchased this book to try and make yourself happy if you didn't love yourself! Read that again! It will not be hard at all because you already have a safe landing space. You become your own safe landing space. When you are not sure about what to do, ask yourself. File it away and wait a few days. The answer will more than likely come to you on its own. I don't go to other people for advice. I did that for most of my life and it didn't get me where I wanted to be. Not that there is anything wrong with asking others for advice. Also remember that other people's limitations are theirs, not yours. Personally, I have just found that what other people want for me is completely different than what I want for myself. Also, their perceived limitations regarding their own abilities will likely directly influence the type of advice you receive from them. Other people are learning their own lessons, which may not necessarily be for you. Your lessons are your lessons. You came here to learn, grow, and expand! This whole process starts with accepting yourself! Please set down your defenses and open your mind. Come with me on a beautiful journey that I promise will make your life amazing!

Change takes strength and courage. You cannot expect to do the same things you are doing today and receive different results. Before you can change who you are, you first need to become aware of who you are. Go and get your big girl panties because we have a lot to discuss!

CHAPTER 2
TRUTH, BELIEFS, AND INTUITION

*"Whoever is careless with the **truth** in small matters
cannot be trusted with important matters."*
~ Albert Einstein

The truth is simply **WHAT IS**. But the truth is also a channel inside of you. This channel is connected to your ultimate power or your intuition. There is a part of you that has ALL the answers. All you need to do is tap into it and keep it clear. How do you keep your intuition finely tuned and working perfectly? There are three things you must do. First, you need to always be telling the truth and being authentic. Second, lose your fears. Realize you are source energy and have all you need inside of you already (yes, you are God in a bod)! Third, use trial and error to hear the voice of your intuition. I've always known when someone was lying to me. I could just feel it. I would just get an "icky" feeling that didn't feel right. I didn't realize how strong my intuition already was at that time. I chose to always be honest, not knowing a positive "side effect" would be quicker and clearer access to my inner guidance. This turned me into a human lie detector.

While seeking guidance can be helpful, learning to rely on your intuition is as important in developing your own resilience. Again, there is a time and place for that. For now, focus on listening. Listen to others when they speak, without thinking about what your response will be or what you will do tomorrow. Active listening requires not thinking about yourself. Be present with them in the moment. Act like their words are oxygen and you need them to breathe. Developing your listening skills is a wonderful way to develop your own intuitive abilities. If you can focus enough to truly hear what someone else has to say, there is a good chance you will be able to hear yourself. Meditation helps with this a lot.

You might disregard that still small voice. We all do at first. Differentiating between your own voice and that of higher wisdom can be extremely difficult at first. But don't give up. Your intuition is your biggest ally in life and is the one part of yourself that you really should develop. You will be able to count on yourself for everything and anything. You will know in advance if you are about to make a bad choice, and you can use your feelings to steer you towards what you know to be good for you. When you act in opposition to your "gut," you usually end up paying the price. It's like having a best friend who is a genius living inside of you all the time. It's a friend to tell you when you're making a bad decision, to guide you in the right direction, and to steer you away from danger! You need to learn to trust that inner voice.

Beliefs are your framework for life. You may call it your rule book. You are incredibly powerful! If life were a game, your beliefs would be the rules for your game. YOU set the rules for your life. According to Bruce Lipton in *The Biology of Belief,* researchers say that by the age of seven, we have developed 95 percent of our subconscious mind. Our subconscious mind is basically what runs our life. Over the years, we have accrued beliefs, knowledge, experiences, habits, and feelings that have all contributed to forming who we are, how we think, what we believe, and how we behave. Most of this is on autopilot. You need to become aware of your core beliefs, feelings, choices, and especially your habits. It pays to be mindful. There's a great book about habits called *Atomic Habits* by James Clear. This book has been on the bestseller list for 40 weeks and even made it to number one! Your beliefs can either help you or hurt you. We all have beliefs that do both.

This is great regarding the positive beliefs you have that have helped you in life. But, what about the beliefs you hold that aren't necessarily true? Most times, we aren't even aware of this type of inner programming because it's been there for so long. It's become a part of who we are. Many of these beliefs were created in childhood and some don't even belong to us, but to our parents, and they've been projected onto us! That's why sometimes it's crucial to receive constructive criticism from a third party. You just cannot be overly sensitive to the information you receive. Listen with open ears instead of being defensive. Being able to look at your beliefs with an open mind is a critical element in becoming the person you want to be. Start to question everything. Question your own beliefs and whether they help or hinder. You cannot change what you aren't willing to acknowledge. This all goes back to what I had said in Chapter 1 about being willing to look at yourself differently, or with fresh eyes. It is the only way to identify the changes that you need to make to live the life that you want to live. Awareness is always step one. Just because you believe something, does that necessarily make it true? Beliefs are just thoughts we keep thinking.

Feelings are energy, which are born by your repeated thoughts and impressed by emotion. If you didn't know, thoughts are things, comprised of actual energy. This has been scientifically proven now, so please don't doubt it. Your thoughts are what feeds your mind. Feelings have particular thoughts attached to them that you may not be aware of. In the book *Letting Go* by Dr. David R. Hawkins, this is what he says about feelings and thoughts:

> "When letting go, ignore all thoughts. Focus on the feeling itself, not on the thoughts. Thoughts are endless and self-reinforcing, and they only breed more thoughts. Thoughts are merely rationalizations of the mind to try and explain the presence of the feeling. The real reason for the feeling is the accumulated pressure behind the feeling that is forcing it to come up in the moment. The thoughts or external events are only an excuse made up by the mind."

Your intuition and feelings are intimately connected in a way. The good news is that you can choose how you want to feel. Many people don't believe that and have become victims of their own emotions. But I promise you, all it takes is to make a new choice.

Just one new choice at any given moment and you can choose to stop feeling the pain and to start feeling the joy. If beliefs are the rule book for your life, then, your feelings would be your guidance system along the way. We all need guidance and the kind that comes from within us is the best kind. You can accept guidance from others, but always check with your intuition first to see if it is in alignment with who you are.

I want you to be consciously listening to the voice of your intuition. Unless you have already done some work in this area, you will likely not hear the voice of your intuition. You may choose to disregard it, thinking it to be just another thought in your head. Differentiating between your own voice and the voice of your intuition can be quite challenging. What will likely happen is that you will hear the voice and disregard it. Later you'll realize that it was your intuition attempting to warn you or tip you off. With time, you will start to identify the voice as your intuition and listen to it immediately. When you can do this, you become an immensely powerful force for good. I personally feel the reason we struggle to hear the voice of our intuition is because it does not use words, just feelings. We are not used to interpreting feelings. Fear can also block your intuition, along with any spiritual abilities you may have. Fear really is false evidence appearing real. And we do create our lives through our intentions. Every new thought you think or feeling you feel has the potential to put your life on a completely different timeline or path.

Stop doing things that you don't want to do. We all do things we don't necessarily want to do. I don't mean the daily activities you do to keep a happy and healthy lifestyle, like exercising or going to work. I am referring to the things that impede your progress. Many times, it will be another person asking for a favor. Keep in mind that fine line between helping another and hurting yourself. You cannot give to another that which you don't already possess. It makes sense then to put yourself first and give to yourself first, despite what you have been taught. Our society has sadly taught us to put others first. You cannot afford to do that. Even if you have children, you cannot put on their oxygen mask if yours isn't on, right? Don't waste your time feeling bad about it either.

If someone asks you for help and you can't help, say no! It's not that hard and people do respect you more when you make yourself a priority. If it doesn't feel good or right, don't do it. You will know afterwards, from the outcome, whether you made the right decision. If you continue to go out of your way for others, before taking care of yourself, this work will take that much longer to do.

Making yourself a priority is the foundation of this book and without it, you will not have a leg to stand on.

The people who love you are going to be there for you regardless. Your being able to make yourself a priority and putting yourself first will get you to where you want to be that much quicker. The next time someone asks you for something, and you immediately have a negative feeling about it, ask yourself why? Then be honest with that person and tell them you can't help them. Don't feel the need to offer any explanations or justifications. The words "no" or "I can't" or even, "I don't want to," should suffice. Don't bother to get defensive or nasty. Just show them the new you. The bottom line is always going to be, if it doesn't feel good, don't do it. Treating others better than you treat yourself is putting them on a pedestal. A pedestal, by nature, makes someone higher up than you. It puts you beneath them! You become their fan! Never put any person or desire on a pedestal, as it only serves to push them further away from you.

If you develop your intuition, the rewards will be limitless. I'm using the term "Emotional Sensing System" to identify that part of you—your inner knowing. Your ESS can help you in an unlimited number of ways. Imagine having a little friend on your shoulder who has all the answers to life and knows everything, past and future. Your ESS is another term for your intuition. I also called it your "gut instinct." Your intuition will require you to take some risks along the way in learning to develop it and in recognizing it. Once you begin to identify its voice, you can use it to your advantage in every single area of your life. You will get hunches or urges that defy all rational logic and if you waste time wondering

WHY or needing a reason, you will lose that information! Just trust it! Inspiration can be another form of intuition also.

Eventually, you will be able to ask yourself or your intuition questions about the things you want to know about. The answer might come right away. It may come days or weeks later. Meditation speeds up this process exponentially. Surely, you've heard of the book, *Conversations with God* by Neale Donald Walsch, where he has conversations with God. Anyone can do this! Your ESS is like always having a friend with you, who can get you through anything or help you achieve or be or do anything! I trust my gut down to the tiniest of things because it is the only thing in this world that has never let me down. Imagine how incredible it would always be to have this type of power with you. Work on cultivating your intuition and your ESS. At one point in time, it's going to come down to you needing to count on only you. It feels nice to have others for support, but it's surely no substitute for independence.

Another beneficial thing you can do is to learn to practice the art of silence. There are times to talk, and there are times it's best not to talk. Developing your intuition will help you determine when you should do which. Start to pay attention to how much you talk versus how much you **truly** listen. Most people listen to respond and aren't really listening. Truly listen to people when they talk. Don't feel like you need to always respond. Strive for understanding. Silent or long pauses are a beautiful thing and give both the speaker and listener a feeling of peace and flow. A person can tell when you are actively listening or if you are just waiting for an opening in the conversation to talk about yourself. Act like that person's words are oxygen and you need them to breathe.

Get inside your heart and out of your head. Once you can master the art of listening, being silent more often will become easier for you. Listening to others is great practice for yourself. Listen to them with as much focus and attention as you would like another person to listen to you. Learning to get quiet and listen will help you tremendously to hear the voice of your intuition. Typically, the more intelligent the person, the less they talk. Smart people are usually the quietest. Also, not talking so much makes you appear far more mysterious and there's nothing men love more than trying to figure out a mysterious woman! Talking too frequently can create an intensity that most people in general are just not ready for!

You can learn to be an observer in your own life. Sometimes it is more advantageous to keep some pieces of you to yourself. Not everyone in your life needs to know every little thing about you. Quiet people tend to be more revered and respected. They come off as very mysterious and intimidating. Sharing ideas or new goals or projects that you have in mind might not always be in your best interests. Whenever you are in doubt, just ask your intuition if this person is someone you should be talking to right now. People don't remember what you said or did; they only remember how you made them feel. When people feel heard by you, you become a valuable person in their lives. Imagine how wonderful of a tool this would be to use on a first date.

Why go through all of this? To what end? To change yourself. That is the goal. We want to change you at your core. Your core is your essence, or what you are made up of. It's your identity and your self-concept. Until you change your identity, NOTHING ELSE IN YOUR LIFE WILL EVER CHANGE. It's a culmination of all your thoughts, feelings, dreams, fears, hopes, stories, patterns, and much more. Essentially, it's who you've been programmed to be based on your circumstances. Who are you at your core? Do you know? I had no clue who I was when I began this journey. But as I progressed, I got to know myself more and more. My core identity became solid. After you solidify your core, you can make it glow. When you are unsure of yourself or feel insecure, so is your core. You need to connect to the best feeling thoughts that you always have available to you at any given moment. Your feelings are what alters your energy. Your feelings are energy. Your intuition can become your best friend if you can learn to listen. A great book to read about changing your identity is *Psycho-Cybernetics* by Maxwell Maltz. In this classic, he discusses how everything we think, feel, and do stems from this core identity and it's not something you can fake either. If you have low self-esteem, no matter how hard you try it'll show up in your actions and behaviors. Alternatively, if you have high self-esteem, that will also be evident as well. Energy never lies. Learn to love yourself and if you don't love who you are now, become someone else who you can love! That's actually a secret key to healing illness and disease, because illness and disease can only live in a false self, or one who isn't being who they really are! Connecting with your intuition will help you to know who you really are. And just a helpful side note here; if you're trying to figure out your passion or purpose in life and feel you have no clue what it is, it may be because you have been people-pleasing so long that you lost yourself. You just need to consistently be saying NO to others, which is always saying YES to you.

Sometimes when we feel like we don't know who we are, it's because we're empaths who have spent our entire lives meeting the needs of others. Due to deficits in getting our needs met during childhood, such as being seen, heard, soothed, and nurtured, we met the needs of others for connection instead. All infants and children require those things, along with attachment to parents, and a vast majority of children didn't get these needs met. Now we're a generation of people who don't know who we are or what our purpose is. I promise you, this can all be resolved. You absolutely can be happy, no matter what your childhood or life was like before reading this book!

We all radiate energy from our core. When we are positive, we're said to be filled with light and love. We are always attracting what we are. We don't attract what we want as the law of attraction would suggest. But rather, **we always attract who we are being**! What you think, feel, and do, is who you are being at any given moment. The universe can only read energy, not words. Everything that you say and do will come from your core identity. Everything is feelings. Words are man-made. Your core is who you are on the inside and what you stand for. My wish is that you glow! When you glow, you're experiencing higher energy emotions, such as love, appreciation, gratitude, and joy, on a consistent basis! The universe has no choice but to attract people, situations, and experiences that match who you are at your core. Glow attracts glow! If you are sad or depressed and thinking that things never go right, guess what? That is what you are currently asking for more of, for more things to go wrong. The only way to move from darkness to light is to reach for the thought that feels better. Reach for the light. Start there and start small. Your main objective should always be to feel good at least 51 percent of the time. And when you don't, ask yourself why and what you can do to get back to feeling good. Just keep reaching for a better feeling thought, even if it only feels one percent better. Slow and steady wins the race.

Once you gain control over your thoughts, you can then also have control of your feelings. It is crucial that you get control of your thoughts and feelings if you want to get anywhere in life. We live in a universe of abundance which means you can also experience an abundance of lack or worry. Where attention goes, energy flows. Whatever you put your attention on is what you'll create more of in your life. If you feel like a victim or that life is unfair, you'll attract more experiences in your life that reinforce the belief that "life is unfair." If you believe that we live in a fair universe and believe in good things, good things will come your way. It's always your choice in what you feel, think, and believe. All is fair in love and war!

When your core identity is solid and you are not waiting for any man, **they wait for you.** When you are filled up on the inside, you do not need someone else to fill your cup. You fill your own cup. Constantly looking outside of yourself for the things you need in life will keep you doing just that, always looking outside of yourself. Seeking external validation is a form of codependency and neediness which are both incredibly unattractive qualities to both men and women! Men need to be doing things for you.

The main reason I am so brutally honest is because it keeps my connection to my intuition working and clear. Authenticity is so important. Life is so much better when you always tell the truth. I had been practicing brutal honesty for years before I could hear the voice of my intuition. I go out of my way to never judge people. You need to learn to be more concerned with your own feelings about your appearance than with the feelings of others. And you should love your appearance, flaws and all. I think that we live in an imperfectly perfect universe. Let me forewarn you, sometimes you will have to break a few eggs. Honesty is worth everything. And you can't have a great relationship with a man or anyone for that matter, if it's built on lies. It's totally possible to be honest and kind at the same time. Besides, people like resistance from others. Doormats and pushovers aren't much fun! People like to be mentally challenged and to be put in their place, especially if they're being unreasonable.

Love is so much easier than we make it out to be. If it's too hard, it's not right! Over the years, women have become "people pleasers," who feel the need to do everything for everyone to be liked. Start liking yourself first and doing things for yourself. You will **not** glow from someone else's words or actions. Real glow only happens when you decide to make an investment in yourself. Be complete without another person. The more you can be real and truthful with both yourself and others, the sooner you will begin to glow! Honesty is where it's at! You will not have access to your intuition or be able to change at your core, without doing some self-evaluation. Stop with the victim mindset and look at your life, without so much sensitivity or negativity. If you want to shine from your core, you have to shed years of conscious or subconscious fears. This is where shadow work can help. How do you shine from your core?

CHAPTER 3
AT YOUR CORE –
YOUR IDENTITY

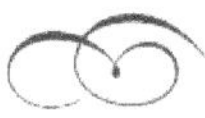

*"You are under no obligation to be
who you have identified yourself to be."*
~ Jeneth Blackert

In Chapter 2, I touched on what your "core" is, but I did not go deep. Your core is your foundation or who you are internally and all-encompassing. Anything and everything that you think, feel, say, or do, comes from your core. It's the center of your inner truth. You need to strengthen your core and increase your light. Please open your mind and let down your walls. I am going to be discussing all the inner qualities that you need to have a solid core. Your identity is who you are internally, and it shows in every little thing you say and do.

Start with self-acceptance. You need to accept yourself right now, flaws and all, as we discussed in Chapter 1. I don't care how unattractive or imperfect you think you are. It doesn't matter if you're thin or overweight, young or old. You're valuable because you exist! Please let that sink in. Most people feel insecure and compare themselves to others. I can assure you that it's NOT JUST YOU! Society has brainwashed the masses into attempting to look and be perfect. If you dare to compare, you will be let down because there are always those both more and less fortunate than you. The only person you should ever be comparing yourself to is your former self. I know how difficult it can be to feel worthy if you never have before. From an incredibly early age, we've all been told what needs to be changed about us, always according to someone else's standards too. It can feel like you are banging your head off a wall, trying to be someone else's ideal. Don't do that! Always know who you are and what you want in life, or you could become susceptible to changing yourself to fit into someone else's ideal of who you should be. You came here to be the unique person that you are, not anyone else's puppet. The opposite of fitting in is standing out and the people who stand out are the people who change the world for the better!

Once I accepted my perceived limitations or weaknesses then I embraced them. If you can do that, you have broken the seal. This is probably the most difficult part of all of this because you have been living safely inside of your own discomfort up until now. A person could be so miserable, but at the same time, so comfortable being uncomfortable that they stay stuck. Emotional pain stinks. But a lifetime of being less than you were meant to be hurts a lot more. If you don't do anything to change your current circumstances right now, what's going to make your tomorrow feel better than today? Absolutely nothing! Decide to BE the change to see a change in your life. Imagine your life five years from now if you change nothing. And how about ten years from now? Start doing the things you would do to be that person you'd like to be now. Ask yourself what habits that person has, who they associate with, and how they spend their time, and then just do it!

Ask a friend or family member what self-imposed limitations they think that you have set for yourself. Don't go into this being defensive or sensitive because you won't get anywhere with it. Personality and **attitude** make a person, not looks. Women gain weight from pregnancies. People get sick and can't move around well. Human beings are constantly changing, and any intelligent person knows that beauty is only skin deep and true love is blind.

Acknowledging and accepting your flaws is essential before moving on. Nobody in this entire world is perfect. Be who you are. You came into this world with unique gifts. You have had unique experiences and there's only one you in this world. Why would you ever want to be like someone else and not embrace and share who you are with the world? Would you really throw away all your originality just to be liked and accepted by people who don't even like or accept themselves? You do yourself a great injustice when you try and "fit in." Please embrace your individuality. Acknowledge and embrace who you are and own your flaws. Love yourself. There is only one you, and I can assure you that you came into this world with a divine purpose that only YOU can fulfill. You can't do that trying to live up to someone else's ideal.

Once you can accept yourself for exactly who you are right now, then and ONLY then, can you fully love yourself. If you are nitpicking about your appearance or feeling unacceptable, then you do not yet love yourself. You have to be the one who accepts and loves yourself before anyone else will. For years I pondered the concept of self-love and wondered what it meant to completely love myself and I thought that I really did love myself. The things, people, and circumstances I was tolerating in my life were huge indicators that I didn't love myself.

We have grown up in a society that has taught us so many mixed messages. We're told to treat others as we would like to be treated. That doesn't mean you should bend over backwards to be there for people who would not do the same for you. You need to put yourself first. If your cup is empty, what do you have available to give to someone else? Somewhere in time, people stopped making themselves a priority. And sadly, the people who end up bending over backwards to help others at their own expense are mainly women! I've read that 80 percent of the people who suffer from autoimmune diseases are women! A big factor in the development of autoimmune diseases is repressing the true self and needs of the individual. Please always be true to yourself and stand up for what you want and need. Practice stating your needs clearly in low-stakes situations to build your confidence in more challenging moments.

If you love yourself at your core, the rest of this book will be so easy for you to understand and put into action. If you find yourself struggling with anything, please come back to this section. The reason I never knew what it really meant to love myself before now was because I didn't love myself. I thought I did. We aren't taught that in this society. Look at your life and the things you are tolerating to determine how much you love yourself. Everything in your life should be simply wonderful! Now that I do love myself, explaining this concept is easy because it's all coming from a very real place. My core identity is love. You can't explain something to another that you don't fully understand yourself!

Loving yourself is so huge. Everything that you do in your life will come from this place. Everything that you do will reflect who you see yourself to be at your core. Loving yourself provides a type of inner security that you cannot get from another person no matter how much you love each other. You are the person that you will be spending the rest of your life with. Anyone else is just a bonus. If you don't love yourself, why should anyone else? Loving yourself gives you a solid core. Difficult choices become that much easier to make. You tend to rely on other people less or not at all. If you are the type to run to others for advice, this will stop as well. Once you love yourself, things kind of just fall into place and everything becomes easier. Someone who loves themselves always respects themselves and has strong boundaries. You cannot love yourself without respecting yourself.

What do you do when other people need your help or want something from you? Will you be hurting yourself to help another? If that is the case, the answer is a resounding NO. You do not hurt yourself to help someone else. Watch that fine line. "Love means to do no harm," as said by Aaron Abke. Never assume that someone else thinks the same way that you do or that they are as thoughtful or compassionate as you are. Don't think they run their lives according to the same standards or moral codes that you live by. Familiarity does breed contempt. Always listen to your intuition. If you're wondering if you should help someone, but it feels like a stretch for you to do it, say no.

Beginning to genuinely love yourself from your core might not be easy especially if you've been hating yourself for most of your life. In the book *You Can Heal Your Life* by Louise Hay, she discusses how all people have some form of self-hatred. So many of us have carried shame or guilt from childhood that we're not even aware of and these feelings reside in our subconscious within our identity. It's literally at the core of our being. Our subconscious controls 95 percent of our life and our identity is a massive part of this! If you haven't heard, our bodies are our subconscious mind, so you need to notice what you're paying attention to and who you're being at all times. Become super aware of everything you think, feel, say, and do. Our awareness (or consciousness) accounts for 90 percent, while only 10 percent of that is dependent upon our action! Just becoming aware of what you really feel about yourself is massively powerful. In the book *Change Your Mind* by RJ Spina, he has an exercise that he personally used himself to get to know himself better. He calls it the "notebook exercise," where he carried around a notebook for 14 days straight and wrote down every single thing he did and then asked himself why he did it, and he was amazed by the results! The example he gives is how one night he woke up and went to the bathroom and automatically started brushing his hair and he had no idea why! His subconscious was doing it. He asked himself, "Why am I brushing my hair?" His mind responded with, "Because I want to look good." And then he asked, "Why do I want to look good?" The answer he got was, "So that other people will like me!" So often we do things without even knowing why we're doing them. It's unconscious. We need to make the unconscious conscious by becoming aware! We need to learn why we do what we do by becoming mindful at all times.

Respecting yourself starts with loving yourself. What does respecting yourself look like and feel like? On the outside, it looks like confidence. On the inside, it feels like pure power. The reason being is that it's an internal strength and reverence for oneself. You hold yourself highly. Those who could once manipulate you, hurt you, or make you feel bad, no longer hold that power over you.

The word integrity simply means doing what is right, all the time, even when no one is watching. For example, a couple years back I was constantly finding wallets chock-full of cash. I always returned them untouched. That's integrity. I would want a person to return my lost wallet. You cannot keep a lost wallet and wonder why no one returns yours when you lose it. I care about doing what is right, just because it's what's right. Ask yourself if you would do that. Respect is another word for value. If you show another person respect, you show them that you value them. Self-respect is valuing yourself. Do you value yourself? How do you treat yourself? Usually, someone with self-respect knows to put themselves and their own needs first. If you are still catering to others, while you know your cup is not full, you do not have enough self-respect.

The bottom line is that we teach people how to treat us by showing them how we treat ourselves. People learn how you feel about yourself and what you are willing to do for them or to tolerate very early on. Always have boundaries and don't allow anyone to cross them. Confidence and respect for oneself cannot be faked. It must be real, and it must come from the inside. Everything comes from the inside and then manifests on the outside. Your external world is a projection of your internal world. Your core is your everything! It is who you are and where all your decisions come from. In the book by Bruce Bryans titled *Never Chase Men Again* this is what he says regarding women and their level of confidence:

> "A woman's confidence is communicated to a man by what she stands for and what she doesn't. Being able to confidently socialize with men, having confident body language, and illustrating confidence in your femininity (in the way you dress and carry yourself) will only go so far if you still allow men to have their way with your emotions, time, affections, body, and anything else for that matter. Self-Confidence makes a woman more attractive, but unless it affects how she enforces her personal boundaries it won't do anything to keep a man interested in her for the long-term."

What he's basically saying is that you need to be constantly and actively enforcing your boundaries with men in order for them to know you're confident enough to take you seriously. You can't create boundaries, not enforce them, and then wonder why a man continually craps all over you. I'm confident enough to make myself a priority and enforce my boundaries. Please be sure to be able to stand strong if you do go on a date. If you don't feel confident enough to leave a bad date, don't go!

Your beliefs need to be brought to your awareness and analyzed. It's your beliefs that define your life and your results. As I've mentioned earlier, your beliefs are your rules for life. They are the rules you've chosen based on your prior belief system, knowledge, and life experience. They also align with your identity. You cannot change what you aren't aware of. If you are stuck in some part of your life, you need new information to become unstuck. Einstein said, "We cannot solve a problem from the same level of consciousness that created the problem." That is my favorite quote in this entire world. That and another famous Einstein quote: "Nothing changes until you do." I know they sound so cliché, but I assure you, they are very valid. Einstein truly was a genius. He understood the outer and inner worlds in ways most people couldn't even fathom. You need to acquire "new consciousness" to get out of any current problems you are facing, which requires a new perspective. Learn to live inside the solution (present) and let go of the problem (past).

You need to be different and see yourself differently!

One topic that I need to address here is that of money. Money is the currency of this realm and is tied to your self-identity. If you have any type of negative emotions connected to money, I suggest you ditch them right now. Money is not good or bad. It's just energy. Our natural birthright is that of abundance, which means abundance is freely flowing to us always. Blocks to your natural flow come in the form of limiting beliefs you have that are untrue. There is absolutely nothing wrong with you and no reason you cannot have an abundant life. If you talk down about people who have money, expect to keep on not having money. You cannot hate something and have it at the same time! Those are mixed messages you are sending out. If you think in terms of lack, you will receive more lack because you are feeling it. On the other hand, if you FEEL abundant, abundance will be your experience.

Your natural state is that of abundance. If you're not currently experiencing that, you need to discover your block(s). You may be experiencing an abundance of lack, in health, in wealth, or in love. **It's an abundance of something you don't want!** The heart is WAY smarter than the brain, despite what you've heard. Google it. It's been proven now that the heart has the same types of cells as the brain. While the brain processes thoughts, the heart deals with feelings and is electromagnetic! Your heart is the most powerful and intelligent organ in your body!

What can you do in this world without money? Maybe thousands of years ago you could survive and thrive, before paper currency. This is the universal currency that we've established for giving and receiving. There's no way around it and to deny that is to deny yourself. Money is power and without it you will struggle. Do what you need to do to ensure that you always have the freedom to choose. Money gives you that freedom. If you can deny that to yourself, you're not ready for honesty. Don't hate the rich. Learn from them. Associate with them. Find out how they think. Be like them and emulate them. Never spend all you earn either. When you have no money, your freedom to dream becomes minimized, because most things in this world seem out of reach. You cannot curse what you want and then wonder why it isn't coming into your life. We all need money in this world. I want you to have every single advantage at your disposal. The amount of money you have is directly tied to your identity, who you feel that you are at your core. Feel rich to be rich!

Start by being grateful for what you have right now. Being grateful now puts you into alignment with the universe (God or Source). You align into receiving mode because you're showing gratitude in advance for what you have and things to come. When the electricity goes out in your house, you're suddenly very aware of how much you use electricity and miss it. Were you ever grateful for it while it was on? Did you acknowledge and feel gratitude for it? Most people don't. We wonder why nobody notices the good we do but gets on our case each time we screw up. But aren't we also guilty of that? How much recognition do you give to the people in your life? How much do you appreciate the blessings in your own life? Do you appreciate the heat that blows right into your home to keep you warm, the running water, the cozy bed, nice clothes, and a properly working body? You won't be given more until you can see what you have already. What are you ignoring right now that you could show gratitude for? The more you are grateful for, the more the universe will give you to be grateful for. It's not a cliché. It's pure alignment with God!

Everything is energy. You and I are energy. Money is energy. How you use it or abuse it will determine how much you have or lack. Think for a minute about how you feel when you have money versus how you feel when you don't. Notice the difference? Money provides freedom. Do you want freedom or imprisonment? Would you like to have choices or be told what you can and cannot do? Being aware is the first step. If you can see it, you can change it. Go and get yourself a surplus of money and never spend all that you have! If possible, always try keeping a $100 bill in your purse that you don't spend just so you can feel abundant. The universe is always matching your current feelings. It would behoove you to feel abundant every single minute of every day. The abundance you experience on the outside in your everyday life is simply a result of how abundant you feel on the inside. No one else is better than you or has anything you don't. They simply made different choices and never gave up. Can you make different choices and choose to never give up?

Who says you must be the person that you were yesterday? For about a month, I had this concept stuck in my head and I just could not verbalize it. Enter Jeneth Blackert on Facebook. She nailed it. She said, "You are under no obligation to be the person that you've identified yourself to be." You are ALWAYS free to choose who you'd like to be. You don't owe it to anyone to be any certain way. This is your life and yours alone to do what you want with it. You can be a lawyer in Boston one day and the next day move to Tibet and become a monk. It's your life and you make the rules. You are in no way obligated to your past personalities, friends, or loved ones, to continue to be an unhappy person or to live a life you are not happy with! If you don't like it, change it! You have all the power to do so.

Once you know who you want to be, consider what it is you would have to do to become that person. What do you want your life to look like? What type of people do you want in it? Where are you living? How are you bringing in money? Are you doing something you love for money? **You must know what you want before you can get it.** You cannot sit around hoping that life will drop a magical miracle into your lap. Once you know what you want, get up and go do something about it. Inspired action is the goal here, not procrastinating motivation. Do anything. Perfection is not a goal. Action is the goal. You must just keep going and fine tuning along the way. If you choose to believe in yourself and never give up on yourself, the universe will support you. Remember, you can be anyone or anything you'd like to be, so choose wisely. I bring up the topic of money in this section on identity because not having money can significantly influence our identities in a very negative way. How can you relax enough on a date if you're worried about being short on rent? Creating an abundance within yourself will become a key part of your identity and you'll easily manifest money and other forms of abundance when your identity feels abundant! Raise your financial thermostat and your self-love thermostat to experience a massive glow up!

This is not something you can fake your way through. Being real, being honest, and helping others, that's all I care about in this entire world. If my only purpose here is to inspire others to be more honest, then I consider that a worthy and noble endeavor and I will fulfill that purpose. The thing is, I really do care about you! You, who is reading this right now. I have been where you are right now, and I do know how badly it hurts. If I can lift myself out of the pain pool, the victim mindset, the people-pleasing, and the living for others, then so can you! But you must be real. You can't play games. Game playing is a temporary fix on a permanent problem or situation. You want to know what kind of women need to play games with men? The women who cannot solidify their cores and don't have a solid identity. These women have not done the inner work and are operating from their unconscious shadow selves (Inner child). They don't set strong boundaries or stand up for themselves. You only have to fake it when it's not real. Choose to be an adult and keep it real. It's the far better choice.

Even with a solid core, you will still have your general problems and bad days. But they will be so much easier to handle if you have this inner strength inside of you. Please nourish yourself and nurture your soul. Do you. Until you become complete within yourself, you will always be looking to someone else to make you feel fulfilled. Put the power of fulfillment into your own hands by taking charge of your life and crafting it to be precisely what you would like it to be. Looking to another person to fill a void you have inside of yourself will only further perpetuate that void in you. I will go into more detail on being complete within yourself before dating another later. For now, practice having every single minute of your life consumed with things that you love to do. Go and treat yourself right now with a hot cup of tea, a bubble bath, or whatever soothes your soul. Why? Because you exist and you deserve it. I want you to feel good before we go on, for no reason, other than that of feeling good. Go now and do what you need in this moment to feel complete.

CHAPTER 4
BE A HIGH-VALUE WOMAN

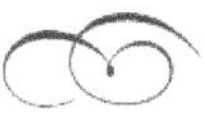

"There is something infantile in the presumption that somebody else has a responsibility to give your life meaning and point. The truly adult view, by contrast, is that our life is as meaningful, as full and as wonderful as we choose to make it."
~ Richard Dawkins

Now that we've discussed the importance of having a solid core identity and the necessary components to having a solid core, we can build on that. Do what you did yesterday and get what you've got today. Do something new today, and you can experience something new tomorrow. Fear keeps you small and stuck. I need you to be fearless. I need you to want to know yourself on a level so much deeper than you do right now. Have a burning desire to intimately get to know yourself. I know this is scary. The unknown is always scary. If you elect to let fear control you, it will. That's its entire job, to control you. It takes time to be able to look at yourself in all of your rawness, without judgment, and say, "Okay, this is working, this is going right, but hey, what's this over here and how well is this working?" If you're more concerned with being right, this won't work. Please throw out your concepts about right and wrong, good and bad. Your ego is not your friend because **its** main job is to keep you safe. I'm not here to judge you. I'm here to love you and help you. Are you also helping and loving yourself? I know you are. If you weren't, you wouldn't have gotten this far in this book because I know this isn't easy to do.

Ultimately, what I really want you to be able to do is to step outside of yourself and see yourself as someone else. And this someone else is nothing but loving. This someone else simply observes, without labeling or judging. You know which aspects of your life are going well and which could use some modifications. Common sense says that you need to learn something new and put it to use in your life to have the life you want to live. How do you do this? You can try doing it by yourself, but, if you haven't been successful changing this in the past on your own, you likely won't be now either. Most of us may need to turn to a friend or family member who knows us well enough to see our problem behaviors and patterns. Try choosing someone who will be both tough and loving with you. I've found that when people are stern with me, in terms of my own self-improvement, I learn more quickly. Sometimes, the insertion of some type of emotional pain tends to make a more lasting impression. But what stings or stays with you more, a random nice comment or someone insulting you? Think about it.

Once you get to truly know yourself, everything will change for you. Your consciousness will have expanded. You will have tapped into more awareness, especially if you can do it in a purely observational manner, by not attaching the meanings of good or bad to any of what you learn about yourself. Absolutely everything is changeable! It won't change until you look at it, though. Being aware or conscious is the key to your transformation. Are you prepared to take a good, long, hard look at yourself—your choices? Your past, present, future? Your habits, fears, beliefs? Your hopes, goals, and dreams? I hope so, because you'll need to. We're not taking the scenic route. I want to get you to where you need to be as quickly as possible.

You'll be asking a **true** friend who loves you unconditionally for help because you genuinely want to become a better you. I would ask multiple friends. You will have the final say regarding what information you accept to be true and what information you consider invalid and disregard. The easiest way to do this is simply to think of the areas of your life that you're unhappy about. Ask your friends what kind of tendencies or patterns they think you may have that could be impeding your progress. A lot of the time you can simply look back at your life at some of the past criticisms you've received and find the validity in those.

Don't defend your limitations unless you intend to keep them. Sometimes, if you've maintained a cordial relationship with an ex-boyfriend that's healthy, you can also ask him. Who better to ask, right? Keep in mind who he is also and where the words are coming from. Do that with anyone you ask for advice from. The most difficult part about this is not getting defensive. If you get defensive, you defeat the entire purpose. Don't make it personal. I know it feels personal but take the personal aspect out of the equation. Basically, this is a fact-finding mission. You want to live a better life than you're currently living, and nothing will change if you don't. If you have no clue where to begin making those changes, how can you change?

Go deep into designing your life, consciously. In the last chapter, we discussed figuring out what you want in your life. I can't stress how important this is. Please don't be one of those people who complains about your life sucking but does absolutely nothing but sit around and wait for things to change. Things don't change by themselves. You change them. When you change internally, only then will things begin to change externally. Never wait for anyone or anything to make your life better. Make it happen on your own. To do that you need to know what you want. You need to determine what it is that you want in your life and then take inspired action towards getting it. Abraham Hicks always says to get "tuned in, tapped in, and turned on," meaning to connect to source. All change starts from within.

No, you don't need to know the exact right thing to do. You just need to do something, anything. You will figure it all out along the way. The Universe always helps too. Determine what you want your life to look like. What do you love to do? What kind of people do you want to have in your life? What is important to you? What excites you and lights you up inside? Where do you want to be a year from now and what are you doing to make that happen? Please take note that the kind of people you surround yourself with will heavily influence the outcome of your life. Try to surround yourself with people similar to the type of person you would like to become. You can't spend all your time with goldfish and wonder why you still aren't a dolphin. Change is hard. Please be gentle with yourself. Figure out what you want your life to look like, down to the last detail. Then take inspired action towards getting what you want. Know that you won't be alone either. The Universe is always supporting you, whether you believe it is or not.

One thing I did a lot of that I want to save you from is taking uninspired action. I would spin my wheels in one direction and then another and I'd never get anywhere! It was because my core identity was completely insecure! Only take action when you feel inspired to! Abraham Hicks talks a lot about "becoming it in your mind first." Many people think Abraham is all about non-action, but that's not the case! It's about taking "aligned action." You have to connect with the source, release your ego, and take inspired action when you feel inspired! Forcing yourself to do some mundane activity as a means to an end rarely gets you to anywhere great.

Our emotions can control a lot of our lives if we allow them to. I need you to be aware of your emotions at all times, so they don't control you. We all have a story. You will need to get a grip on your emotions and drop your story. Your mindset is everything. A high value woman is always in control of her emotions and attitude. She never pities herself either. Being jealous of others, comparing yourself to others, or being envious of others are all symptoms of fear. You automatically disempower yourself whenever you blame a person or a situation for making your life the way that it is. If you have no control over something, you can't change it! Let it go!

How do you get control over things in your life that are within your control? You take responsibility for all of it. You must do this to move forward, no matter how much you may not like it. Your thoughts have been the precursor to everything you've ever experienced in your entire life. While the incident that happened may not have been your fault, the way you reacted to it **is** within your control. Take responsibility for your entire life, but don't actually "blame" yourself for anything, because you were always doing the best you could in the moment. I want you to continue to treat yourself with love, kindness, and compassion. You can't change a thing until you take responsibility for it. Blaming others will always keep you stuck because you can't change other people. Forgive, let go, and move on.

If you continue to blame your parents, family, friends, your boss, or your boyfriend, your situation will remain the same, stuck in blame. Take responsibility for every little thing in your life, even if deep down you feel it's not on you. **This is the only way that you can change it.** Taking responsibility for things is taking your power back. Own up to your own part in any misery you may have experienced. How could you have chosen to feel differently? And don't say that you can't help how you feel because we all know that's a cop-out. You choose your thoughts. Repeated thoughts with attached emotions create lasting feelings. Feelings also have a lot of thoughts attached to them. You created your situation, like it or not. And only you are choosing to perpetuate it. Where your attention goes, your energy flows. Where are you directing your energy? Are you headed towards the problem or towards a solution? The answer lies in your thoughts. Thinking about the problem at all only perpetuates the feeling of being a victim and changes nothing and keeps you in those old negative emotions. If you keep your thoughts on a solution instead of escaping thoughts of victimization, that is the first step in the right direction! In the book *Don't Believe Everything You Think*, Joseph Nguyen goes onto say how we really don't even need to think at all. Our natural state is one of meditation. Our subconscious knows everything we need to do and does it naturally. Just imagine how much thinking has gotten in your way.

The most difficult and time-consuming part of this work is altering your beliefs. We all have so many limiting beliefs in place, most that we're not even aware of. Our subconscious mind is what runs us when we're on autopilot and controls our thinking and habits. It's what regulates our breathing and other involuntary activities happening inside of us. It keeps us safe and alive. Only five percent of our conscious mind is available to us after age seven. This means that, no matter what age you are right now, you're likely still running on the basic programming of a seven-year-old! Up until age seven, our brains are in the theta state, a hypnosis state. Your habits come from your subconscious mind. Think about how many things you were told as a child and expected to believe and likely did. Consider the things you were taught as a child as well. These beliefs are so deeply ingrained in us that we aren't even aware of who we are. Some beliefs are good and there to help us, but not all of them are helpful. What if the original beliefs that you had aren't serving you, but hurting you? How do you change that? You change by becoming aware of it. Let's practice. You must find out what it is about yourself that you don't know (awareness). This involves digging into your shadow or spending time with your inner child, which resides in the subconscious mind. Our shadow side or inner child are parts of ourselves that have not been seen, heard, soothed, or nurtured, including the parts of ourselves we've ignored to connect more with others. Working on my inner child is the most beneficial work I've ever done in my entire life.

We will do this exercise together, so you can begin to understand how to disintegrate a false belief system. As far as dating goes, we all have different beliefs, based on what we've learned, been told, seen happen to others, and experienced ourselves. This is the belief system that you have chosen to adopt. Let's say that you're 50 years old and you feel that no man wants someone who is 50. This is an opinion, not a fact. If you adopt that idea into your belief system, it will become a reality for you! You might even stay home all the time and miss out on potential opportunities to meet interesting people because of your false belief. And if you do go out, you won't meet anybody. On the flip side, you can be 80 years old and go around telling everyone how much you love yourself and love life and every man in the free world wants you. Who do you think will be living the reality that they've created for themselves? Both women will! Your belief is true because you believe it to be so. A belief is simply something you have chosen to accept for yourself. Why would you adopt a belief that is negative and hurtful? Can you see what I mean about loving yourself now, and why it's so important? The 80-year-old woman loves herself and believes in herself, while the 50-year-old woman doesn't. See the difference? You can choose the empowering belief or the disempowering belief. Which would you rather have? I'd rather be the 80-year-old woman who believes anything is possible than the limited 50-year-old. Our beliefs create our lives. We magnetize people to us who have the same energy we do!

Our challenges repeat themselves until we learn the lesson they're trying to teach. In this scenario, what's going to stop the 50-year-old from continuing to have this false belief? Her awareness of it and hopefully her invalidation of it! She also must make a commitment to change. If she wants to be in a relationship, she has to believe a new belief about herself. Find the false beliefs that are not serving you and detach your emotions from them. You may need to dig deep into your childhood or do a lot of work with your shadow or inner child to see what beliefs and pain they're carrying.

If you can see the false belief, you can squash it. All it takes is an awareness of it and a desire to let it go. That's the easy part. Finding the beliefs may prove to be somewhat challenging, depending on how long you've had them and how much you're aware of their existence. Decide what new and empowering belief you would like to establish in its place. How about something like, "I'm amazing and everyone everywhere wants to be with me or near me?" It only needs to FEEL believable to you. If it doesn't feel believable or achievable, your mind won't accept it as true, so make sure it feels real. Maybe start small, and say, "I only *feel* old, I'm actually quite young, fun, and interesting!" Just make sure it's something you truly do feel, or it won't work. Search through your beliefs about men and relationships. What stories are you telling yourself? What beliefs do you have about men and relationships? Are they healthy beliefs or unhealthy beliefs? Are they even true? How are they serving you? How much of its purely from your own experiences with men? Do you see other women experiencing this as well or something different? One popular exercise I use with my clients is to have them write down all their negative beliefs about men and disintegrate them!

When I really need an answer to a question and have no one to ask, I ask myself. Usually, in about two days, the answer just kind of "drops into my head." I can be in the shower or daydreaming, and it just comes to me. If you can connect with your own intuition, this will be much easier. Things like this will start happening if you believe they're possible. Embrace it. You're becoming powerful. If you don't believe that something is possible for you in your own life, it isn't. Have you heard the saying, "Whether you think you can or think you can't, you are correct?"

Take a good look at the women in your life. Which of them has a healthy attitude towards dating and relationships? Better yet, who is already in a healthy relationship? Think about your past relationships. I'm sure you can see the pattern. We all have our own patterns. When you are constantly looking outside of yourself for validation, you have a hollow core and an empty identity. If you go on social media and see these women that post nothing but post after post about needing and wanting love, they have hollow cores. Instead of doing the inner work that they could be doing to fulfill themselves, they'd rather find a quick fix in a relationship. These people don't want to face themselves and become codependent as a distraction. As sad as it seems, these relationships almost always fail because the woman isn't really bringing very much into the relationship, other than her own needs. Additionally, someone who is this needy will likely also attract someone who is also very needy as well. This can strain a relationship in unforeseen ways. Doing inner work is so important to attracting and maintaining a healthy relationship.

What is your pattern? Do you date guys with addictions? Maybe you've dated a surplus of guys who never work or have any money? Another common theme is attracting cheaters. Then there's your beaters, abusers, users, and losers. Then you've got your married men who haven't stopped dating yet. Of course, there's also guys who can't commit and those who can't grow up. Until you make a conscious choice to find out what your dating pattern is and destroy it, it will continue to play out in your life. Things happen for a reason and **that reason is always to learn a lesson**. Your life experiences will continue to repeat themselves until you learn what you need to from them and make a conscious decision to heal them. Learn the lesson and you don't need the experience anymore. You take yourself with you into every relationship that you have. If you'd like the dynamic of it to change, it's going to have to start with you.

Some fears are necessary to keep us safe. Most fears only serve as a control mechanism to keep you right where you are. Human beings fear change and the unknown more than anything. People tend to fear what other people think of them too. Many people worry about being loved and accepted. I shudder to think about how many people are ignoring their amazing and unique gifts to appear to be "normal" and fit in with "everyone else." Some people were meant to stand out and not to fit in. Please always be real and be yourself. Most people don't even like themselves. Don't lessen yourself for anyone or anything. The most liberating thing I've ever done in my entire life was to stop caring about what other people think. When you stop focusing on what other people think, you have more time to think thoughts for yourself, about yourself. You make choices based on your desires, not the desires or needs of others. Don't let anyone live in your head rent free! When you live your life for you and stop caring about the opinions of others it's the most freeing thing in the entire world!

Be fearless and you will move mountains. Be the lion, not the sheep. Take control of your life. How would you live your life if it was only about you? I mean, if there was no opposite sex, no romantic love, no marriage or babies. In a world full of women, offering all our current world has to offer, minus all men, what would you be doing with your life right now? That's what you should be doing! Take control of your life. Learn to fulfill your own needs. Looking to others to fulfill basic needs for you will keep your core hollow. Be a woman of substance. Not needing a man in your life is probably the biggest turn on there is for a man. It's all about what's going on inside of a person—their attitude. Our life force is energy. People can sense the energy of others. Are you living a life of your own design, or are you living a life of necessity? You want every part of your life to be created by you. And in time, you can make that happen with an open mind.

Take all men off their pedestals and know that anyone who gets you is the real winner. Make your desires feel within your reach, natural, and easily accessible. Be sure to make it equal to your own self-image and don't put anyone on a pedestal. Things are only impossible if you tell yourself that they're impossible. There's nothing I love more than stretching myself. It feels so amazing. I know that there's so much that I don't yet know or that I have yet to experience and that's what keeps life fresh and interesting! Now I know that the sky is the limit. That impossible dream that I thought wasn't achievable, it's very possible. I can't help but ask myself, what else can I do now? The absolute best you can see for yourself, most likely is not the best you can get. Keep reaching, stretching, striving, and expanding. Kick that ceiling. Not even the sky is the limit here. I want you to dream big, bigger than you ever have before! What's better than the best you've been able to imagine? Go after your highest excitement with a fervent passion!

CHAPTER 5
HABITS TO LOSE

"It is easy to live for others, everybody does.
I call on you to live for yourself."
~ Ralph Waldo Emerson

If I could get my hands on a time machine and I only had one thing that I could go back in time and tell my past self, it would be this: Go out and make something of yourself because time changes nothing; only you do. I remember thinking that my life was out of my hands or beyond my control. I thought there was some "master plan" for how my life would magically work out. I guess you could say that I believed in fate a little too much. I seriously thought that it would all just magically fall into place and that everything I'd ever wanted would just somehow fall into my lap. I think that a lot of us think this way. I truly feel that we're brought up to think that way. Don't wait for people to change or to care more. Stop expecting things to change on their own. Don't look for sympathy from others. It's crippling. People will feel bad for you for a little while, then, you just become a thing of the past. People will move on with their lives and not think twice about you. Use your time to make something of yourself. Things are the way that they are for a reason. You have challenges in your life so that you can rise above them. It's in the rising above that you solidify your core identity. The actual "stuff" that you go through, that's precisely what your character is built upon. As everyone always says, it really is about the journey! It's always about the journey because the destination is at the end and isn't nearly as important. **People in general, and especially men, don't appreciate getting something for nothing!**

One mistake that I've personally made too many times to count, is running back to ex-boyfriends and settling. I did it out of sheer loneliness. These can be two separate things or one in the same. Going back to a relationship that already didn't work out, or that your heart wasn't in 100 percent, is going backwards—and that's settling. Meeting someone new who you aren't that crazy about and continuing to see them, that's also settling. When you settle, you're telling the Universe (God, Source Energy), that this is what you want! You're accepting something that's less than what your heart truly desires. No one is going to come and serve you up a better boyfriend or a better life. That's up to you to do. The only one who will know if you are choosing to settle or not is you. You stop trying to be the best you can be and excel in your life because you've found someone and you're not alone anymore. You get comfortable, despite the obvious discomfort you feel. Please, be picky. Get VERY comfortable with yourself, learning who you are, what you love, what you want to create in your life, and especially what you're unwilling to accept. Being lonely, needy, or desperate can cause you to settle for anyone to avoid being alone. FACE YOURSELF. Feel your feelings too. If you tend to settle to not be alone, chances are super high that you need to do some work on your inner child. Our inner children are alive in us throughout the course of our entire lives! Their unmet needs are what make up what we call our "shadow side." Tons of people are coaching people in shadow work these days and there are journals you can purchase to do shadow work. You can find tons of free resources online to work with your inner child or shadow self.

Only you know what type of person you'd thrive with. You need to know what you're looking for. Have high standards. Too many women seem to jump at the first man who gives them the slightest bit of attention. Then these women jump through hoops for these random guys! When this happens, I feel like their insides are just screaming, "Validate me!" A man is not there to punch your parking ticket. A quality man needs a quality woman. A woman of quality knows she is such and does not need a man to validate her. Please strive to be a woman of quality. Don't pick low hanging fruit. If you're looking to a man to complete you, your relationship is not likely to work out. You can't go into a relationship with a "lack" mind set of, "Please fulfill me!" Basically, you're looking to another person to make you feel whole because you haven't been able to do it yourself. That puts an immense strain on a relationship and if you don't think that the other person can feel it, think again.

I know that being alone can really suck at times. Would you rather be alone for a few months and "do you" and then find the man of your dreams? Or would you rather settle with whoever and put off improving your life just so you're not lonely? How much time are you going to waste with Mr. Wrong before you realize that you're better off on your own? A few months? Maybe a year or two? Time flies. You can waste precious months, possibly even years, with the wrong person, waiting for the right person. You can put your order in with the Universe, providing it is that you already know what you want. You must know what you want before you can get it. If you settle for less than what you really want, you only hurt yourself. Men from the past should stay there. There are always exceptions, people who have turned their lives around or became better people. I will let you be the judge of that. It's your life. Listen to your gut.

We are always learning, growing, changing, and evolving. Dating a "broken man" will take a toll on you in many possible ways. When I say "broken," I mean, he's not living up to his potential. The bottom line is that he is needy and not a divine masculine. Men who can't take care of themselves, let alone a female, are most likely in their wounded feminine energy. We all have both feminine and masculine inside of us. Whether his mom kicked him out at age 15, hoping for greener pastures with her own Mr. Wrong, or he has a notebook full of problems he created for himself, he is a fixer upper. Is that what you're looking for—a project? Someone to acknowledge your existence and come to lean on you for either emotional support, or to maybe even financially support him? Possibly even both. Either way, it's going to take a toll on you.

In the beginning, it might be nice to have someone there, or possibly even be fun, interesting, and exciting. But, if in time, you notice that your own needs are being suppressed, you're with a fixer upper. We attract who we are being. Chances are, if you're dating a toxic male, you're likely a toxic female. That simply means that you're unhealed in some unconscious way. Many of us begin this way and evolve with experience. This is why I say, DO YOU. Spend the time you have to be alone and single doing you. You may very well have the rest of your life to be part of a couple, so why not enjoy yourself now? If dating broken men appears to be a habit for you, you really need to reexamine your patterns in dating. Until you make a conscious choice to change things, you will continue to attract the same kind of men into your life that you always have. Everything is a lesson and once you learn the lesson or heal that part of yourself, you no longer need to relive the experience. Discover your pattern and break it. Never accept less than the best, because you're so worth it!

The best way to gauge anything in your life is to ask yourself how it feels. Your opinion is really the only opinion that matters. If it feels good, hey, rock on! But, if not, you need to make some changes. How are you showing up in your relationships? Are you constantly going out of your way for men? If so, please stop. Seriously! It's such a common misconception that doing things for men will make them like you. It's the complete opposite. Doing things for men will make you look pathetic, desperate, and unappealing. In time, they'll come to take you for granted as well. Think about it. Can you see a classy woman jumping through hoops for a man? No. You will never ever see that. You know why? Classy women respect themselves and know about men. They know what makes them tick. They know that men appreciate absolutely nothing that's handed to them! If you go out of your way for a man, he will not appreciate you! You will become commonplace, like every other desperate female that he has already crossed paths with. You need to know and believe that high-value men do exist if you want to meet one.

If you feel an instant and unexplainable chemistry with a man, chances are the reason for that is because you both experienced similar wounds in your childhood. Real and lasting true love doesn't necessarily start off with a bang. It's usually slower to develop, but it endures. There's not a whole lot that men can do for us that we can't already do for ourselves or pay someone else to do. Let them jump through hoops for you. Men like to feel useful, needed, and manly in a world where we no longer need them for survival. In all honesty, there are many things I can't do for myself that having a man around for comes in quite handy! You can still learn to appreciate the opposite sex without being codependent on them.

Never be attached to anyone. It'll cause you to do things you normally wouldn't do. Desperation and clinginess are huge turn-offs as well. Any inner needs that you have, you should be taking care of those on your own. A relationship should add to your life, not make it complete. You need to be complete within yourself already in order for a wonderful relationship to thrive. How many times have you had one of your girlfriends call you up about the same deadbeat guy she's been with forever? You know he's wrong for her. You know she can do better. It's painful to watch her chase this jerk who doesn't deserve to be in the same room with her. Your friend can't see her own value. Many of us go through this.

Chances are more than once, we too, have tortured our girlfriends discussing some guy we thought was amazing that turned out to be less than wonderful! So, remember that when dealing with your female friends. Show mercy and compassion, to a point. But also know, you don't need to continue to listen to her destroy herself. If your friend is acting desperate and pathetic, chances are she will learn that lesson on her own. When you feel like you're lucky to be with the guy you're with or that he's "too good" for you, you will do too much for him and will end up sabotaging the relationship. You will kill the relationship before it even begins. **A man should feel privileged to be with you**. You are the prize, not him. Never jump through hoops for a man. If you find yourself in a relationship that isn't fair or equal and you know you're doing more work to maintain the relationship, change your behaviors. Things will continue to stay the same until one of you wakes up. Most times talking to men never results in change, not unless you've been together for a long time and have a deep bond already. Men respond much better to action than to words. Show them, don't tell them.

If you're in a relationship right now, I want you to take stock of that relationship. If not, think of the last relationship that you were in. How does or did it make you feel? Do you feel like you're doing most of the caring and the work? Or do you have an equal and supportive partner that you know will be there for you, who makes your life easier and better? The only person who can determine your value is you. If you were needy and pathetic yesterday, choose to stand strong and be independent today. Who do you think determines who you are? YOU DO. Is this guy everything you ever wanted, and then some? If he isn't all you ever wanted AND MORE, then, he isn't good enough for you! If you're unhappy, he's not for you. Either way, it's up to you to choose to stop being a victim and want more for yourself. You can't stop being a victim until you realize you're victimizing yourself! Awareness is half the battle. The first step to not feeling like a victim is to focus more on what you're grateful for in your life rather than the things you don't like or want to change. Be more positive than negative, all the time. Become consciously aware of what you focus on and how you speak to other people. Many people have a victim mindset and are completely unaware of it. And this only perpetuates and brings these people more circumstances, events, and people that make them continue to feel like a victim!

When you stop doing things for men a funny shift happens. They begin to do things for you. Right now, you may be thinking to yourself, "Who me? A man has never." Well, that's because you've never let him! As women, we have some innate part of us that feels compelled to take care of everyone and everything. Being child bearers makes most of us nurturers. Growing up, we're taught to be there for everyone and to treat others as we would like to be treated. Well, that's one saying I'd like you to take with a grain of salt. Never put someone else ahead of you or your own needs. People, even those you love who love you, will see a deficit within you when you're constantly going out of your way for them. Do you know why? They sense that you aren't valuing yourself. When you don't value yourself, other people tend to not value you either. The more I did for a person, the less they respected me. Yes, that's how life REALLY works. Even with the best intentions, people will still take you for granted if you show them that you aren't valuing yourself. Boyfriends, friends, and family will all exploit you. I promise you. And when you start telling people no, they will begin to respect you. Get very good at saying NO to others and YES to yourself. That's a game changer right there.

One thing I can't stress enough is to not have any attachments. If you attach yourself to a person, you have no choice but to tolerate any poor behavior from them that comes your way. You may be very surprised at the man who shows up embodying everything that you love. He can be a million times better than the guy you're with or wanting to be with right now. In fact, so much better to the point that you may want to kick your own ass for not stepping up sooner! How will you know how amazing that new guy is if you're still stuck on someone else who makes you miserable. Please recognize that if you're currently in a long-term unsatisfying relationship.

Men live to please you, whether you know it or not. It gives their lives purpose and meaning. Cleopatra had the right idea. She had men feeding her, massaging her, and worshipping her. Cleopatra was a natural seductress. Her core identity was very solid. She knew who she was, and she embraced it. You don't need to be a Queen or rule a land to get men to jump through hoops for you. All you need to do is ask. That's it, just ask. Of course, you must stop doing things for them. They won't suddenly start waiting on you hand and foot if you've been tending to their needs from the start. This is why I say, never get too attached. You can know the kind of man you want or the type of job you'd like, but don't get stuck on a certain person or place. This is where a lot of your power lies, in your ability to be open.

Liking, loving, or feeling attached to a man who is unhealthy for you stems from some trauma you've experienced in your childhood usually. So, look at **what** it is that you want and leave the specifics to the Universe. It's fun too, getting to see just how much men will do for you. You see women in these wonderful relationships and think to yourself, "Oh, that's never going to happen to me." Well, only because you just said so! No other woman is better than you or has more of anything than you have right now. You deserve everything and more. Men care a lot more about your attitude than your looks. In the big picture, your personality is what will keep the right guy around. You've got to love yourself way more than you love him, and he needs to know that when push comes to shove, you will always choose yourself over him.

You know that one guy you dated? You know, the one who said he wasn't ready for commitment and then you saw a giant rock on his new girlfriends' finger three months after you two had broken up? When a guy says, "It's not you," I can assure you, it is you. Sorry to be the one to break it to you. You gave too much too soon and didn't value yourself enough. Of course, there can be other reasons for the relationship ending. The woman he met right after you (or during), she loved herself and he felt it. Men love being with strong women. They love a challenge, as all people do. Your outer appearance won't matter here. Telling yourself that you're prettier than her doesn't make you feel any better either, because she's got him, and you don't. It just goes to show how little appearances matter in the big picture. Don't get me wrong, I hope you won't leave the house looking all frumpy now. Have some dignity and respect for yourself. Your appearance is how you choose to represent yourself to the world. We will discuss that in more detail in a later chapter. Appearances matter but they're not the end all be all when it comes to love. But for now, please test my theory!

Make up your mind to be someone else tonight. If you're usually a shy and quiet homebody, go spruce yourself up and hit the town tonight. Decide what activities you love or things you enjoy doing and go to public places where others are doing those things! It's really that simple. I don't advocate going to bars. The bar culture is typically just people who work, drink, and fool around. They're usually not serious about wanting to be in a relationship. I want you to go out and experiment with being sociable. Be someone who has always loved herself and expects men to jump through hoops for her. Don't offer to buy anyone anything or do anything for anyone. Let them all do things for you. And if it doesn't happen tonight, work on yourself some more and continue to experiment. Experiment socially with people who are really of no consequence to you. Pretend to be someone charismatic and fun! Glowing from your inner core causes others to be highly attracted to you. Men want to date you, and women want to be you or be close to you. Either way, life is better. It's your light. Let it shine!

This may feel strange at first, especially if you're in the habit of giving so much more than receiving. That's how it was for me at first because I'd always been the one to do for and give to others. It can literally feel uncomfortable because you're not used to it. The part of you that feels discomfort is the old you clinging to old ways of devaluing yourself. You have yet to realize your value, but you will. Continue to work on yourself and continue to raise your standards. It may not feel real at first but if you keep it up, it will become real. Receiving can be hard when you're not used to it. If receiving from others feels uncomfortable for you, please continue to work on yourself until it feels natural. Men want to adore you. Again, this is likely connected to childhood wounds that you're unaware of! Working with your inner child is the most life-changing thing you can ever do! Men can't adore you, until you adore you!

When you realize your value, it'll be automatic that you will simply stop going out of your way for other people. You need to put yourself first and protect yourself. As cruel as it sounds, we do live in a dog-eat-dog world, and everyone needs to be there for themselves first. As women, we tend to be there for others before being there for ourselves though, don't we? Stop suffering to put a smile on someone else's face. Again, there's a very fine line between helping someone else and hurting yourself. Don't skate anywhere near that line. If someone needs your help and you'll be losing something valuable to help them, just say no. People get scared that a person won't like them anymore if they say no. People actually like you more when you say no! If a friend stops talking to you because you didn't do what they'd asked, that person was never a friend to begin with! Read that a few times, because as alarming as it is, it's true. Having people like this leave your life is a huge gain for you! A person who truly cares about you will be understanding and not have unrealistic expectations about your relationship or friendship. In any good relationship, both people are equally present for one another and contribute equally to maintaining a connection.

One topic I need to bring up now is that of guilt. When someone wants something from you that you're not willing to give, they may play the guilt card. Toxic people will attempt to make you feel bad for not being there for them. Remember that how you feel is always *your* choice. I don't entertain this type of behavior at all. I'll literally call a person out on it and ask them, "Are you attempting to emotionally manipulate me?" My favorite thing is when someone wants an explanation for something. You don't need to be explaining yourself to anyone ever. These people used to irk me the most. Funny thing is, it's always the people who don't explain themselves to you. They want to know where you were, why you didn't text back, or pick up the phone. Please don't give away your power by bothering to explain yourself to these people. You don't owe them any explanation of what you were doing with your time. You can't be afraid to lose people either. Let them go. If you're paying my bills, ask away. If not, go away. Explaining and complaining are both habits you definitely need to lose! Both stem from fear and negativity and are only attracting more fear and negativity into your life.

You do need a certain amount of inner strength to be this person and live this life. Plan to make some enemies along the way too because the people who haven't changed like you have just yet, they won't understand the person you're becoming. Some people in your life may prefer the weaker version of you. This is because these people are typically weaker themselves. Change scares them. It scares most people. Change, the unknown, and death are named the top three fears in the world! Get over those and it's smooth sailing from there! Life can become a playground just for you, where you watch all your heart's desires come to life, as if by magic! The power is within you. Never allow yourself to feel guilty enough to help someone else or do anything that you don't want to do! Notice their attempt at this beforehand and beat them at their own game. Trying to make someone do something for you with guilt is something only weaker human beings do. Make note of which people in your life treat you this way and be prepared. Also, be aware of narcissists, sociopaths, and psychopaths. These three types of people generally don't feel empathy and are always takers. If you're with one of them, it's quite likely that you're an empath who is a giver by nature! The predator and the prey. Don't be prey for men like this. Be strong on your own.

Please note that I am not advising against helping other people. I help people all the time, but I only do it when I genuinely want to, and I never expect anything in return. Keeping score or doing things out of obligation can put a huge strain on a relationship. Don't do it in the hopes that one day they'll do the same for you. We usually do get the help we need, but not always from those we'd expect it from. Only give and help from a place of having a genuine desire to do so. It has a lot to do with your own inner strength and your ability to stand as your strongest self.

In the book *Why Men Love Bitches* by Sherry Argove, she discusses just how little you should be doing for men. She states that, "If, after some time, he ever slips and asks you to cook, simply offer to make your specialty: popcorn, wieners, and a jelly roll, with coffee and Kool-Aid to help wash it down. Then start getting ready because you'll have reservations within the hour." I love that quote! She discusses how you boil the hot dogs, slice them up like appetizers, stick toothpicks in them and serve them with some gourmet dipping sauces of ketchup and mustard! She also states that, "The bitch is not the woman who will sit at home and work overtime to refine her 'man-catching' skills. All she feels she has to do in the beginning is focus on being good company." It's that simple. Less is always more when it comes to men. Never go out of your way for a man. If this is a habit you currently have, lose it!

CHAPTER 6
FILL YOUR OWN CUP FIRST

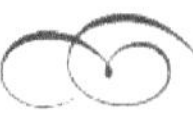

"To be happy, we must not be too concerned with others."
~ Albert Camus

I have been hearing a lot of people saying, "Fill your cup first." We may think our cup is already full, but many times it's not. Having a full cup means that you have plenty of time, money, and energy for yourself. Sometimes helping others is really a distraction from taking the time to look at your own life and make improvements. Our bleeding hearts so badly want to help others to make their lives better, but we haven't bothered to stop and fix our own lives first. It's always harder to help ourselves because it requires getting uncomfortable—and we hate being uncomfortable. Is your cup running over? Do you have more than enough time, money, fun, friends, hobbies, love, and happiness? We care too much about others and not enough about ourselves. We can blame society for how we've been raised, but that's a very disempowering thought.

Remember what we've discussed about blame and responsibility? If every person in the world took it upon themselves to become the very best version of themselves, we wouldn't need to worry about focusing on others as much as we do. The whole world would be healed. Start by identifying one area of your life that needs improvement, and commit to making small, consistent changes every day. If you're an empath, know that you are an energetic food source for narcissists, sociopaths, and many other colorful characters. If you're not an empath, or have never heard of this concept before, an empath is a person with the ability to feel what other people are feeling. Everyone in existence is capable of this. Most times, this ability was developed in childhood because your parents weren't able to meet your needs of being seen, heard, soothed, and nurtured, so you adapted and learned how to figure out what other people needed in order to give it to them for connection. A famous doctor named Gabor Mate discusses in the book *The Myth of Normal* about how all children have two primary needs: the need to be authentic and the need for attachment. If being authentic doesn't get your need met to feel connected as a child, you will begin to search outside of yourself for a way to meet the need of others so you can experience connection with them, if not your parents. And if your needs aren't met, you will sacrifice your authenticity in exchange for a connection with others. Wounded feminine men love to feast on empathic energy from a masculine woman. You can feel it, too. Pay attention to which people make you feel lighter and joyful versus which people drain your energy.

How do you fill your cup first? You take care of your own needs, on your own. If you need to feel loved, YOU give yourself that love by going within yourself and feeling love inside your heart. Do things that you enjoy and make yourself happy in any way you possibly can. You are your own love generator. After that, you can call your grandma or your neighbor or go make new friends or go buy a cat. Don't go to a bar and have a one-night stand or find a new boyfriend to scratch your lonely itch, not if you want a better future. Giving in to current emotional whims in this way will leave you feeling lousy down the road. Learn how to be your own best friend for now. Don't depend on others if you don't have to, not for anything at all, unless you truly have no choice. For most things in your life, you should find a way to be able to count on yourself to fulfill your every need. Only this is true freedom. When you don't need anyone else for anything in your life, you're now free to make your own choices. Stop worrying about your friends and their problems. Fix your own life and your own problems before trying to help others.

Is everything in your life precisely as you would like it to be? Do you have a warm and comfortable home? Do you make enough money to sustain both your needs and wants? Do you look forward to your work each day or do you dread waking up every morning? These are all the things you should be considering. Having a full cup is about your awareness of your own life, being focused on all that you have or the positives in your life. Your life should be full of wonderful things and people. Ask yourself how happy you are within each area of your life, and what you can do to improve in those areas. Until your cup is running over, stop making it your mission in life to help others. Help yourself first. Overflow your own cup. Then pour into the cups of others when you feel like it of course!

Like we discussed earlier, your beliefs are your rule book for life. Whatever you believe, you allow in. Whatever you disbelieve, you disallow. It's that simple. Opting to believe in yourself and your own abilities is the most profound thing you could ever do for yourself and for the world. Sometimes it seems so easy to believe in others but not quite so simple to have that very same faith in ourselves. If your belief is what makes something so, why not make a choice in your own favor and put your faith in yourself? Don't let hang ups from the past impede your progress. Please don't use other people's standards or measurements for progress as your own. Know that you are capable of absolutely anything you desire. The only thing that makes something become impossible for you, is you. It's all about choice. You have free will to do as you choose. Ask yourself now, what do I choose to believe about myself? And then ask yourself, why do I believe in these things? Is it helping me or hurting me to have this belief? All you need to do is take inspired action in the direction that you'd like to go. Travel towards your highest excitement in life! It must be an inspired action though.

When you take **inspired action**:

- You get an impulse or idea to do something, which usually comes to you naturally, easily and often at an unexpected moment.
- The **action** steps just make sense. You don't have to justify them.
- You feel energized by the **action** - it isn't "work."

Believing in yourself, with some excitement about the future is another way to describe inspired action. It doesn't feel like work, more like fun. On the other hand, attempting to motivate yourself into doing something means that it's something you already didn't want to do. Follow your highest excitement to reach your dream life. Before you set off on any endeavor, make sure you are backing yourself 100 percent. It's great to have others there to believe in you, but you need to believe in yourself most importantly. Look at the people who are offering criticisms you didn't ask for. Ask yourself where it's coming from. Is it coming from a genuine place of them caring about you, or are they deflecting the heat from themselves?

Most people have no clue what they're doing in their own lives, so, don't go to others for help or advice, unless you're completely desperate and know someone you can count on to be there for you and your best interests. Your own belief in yourself will be what drives you throughout the rest of your life. You can depend on yourself. You need to believe in yourself and your ability to create the life you've always wanted. Never look to another to tell you that you can or cannot do something. If they say that you can't, it's because it's THEIR own limiting belief in themselves and has absolutely nothing to do with you! You can do it! Just try, and never stop trying. When you believe in yourself and never quit, you learn that there's not anything you can't do or figure out how to do. You become mighty powerful. However, you have to have an identity of confidence and believing in yourself. Others will see you the same way you see yourself and treat you accordingly.

Several times now, I've mentioned the idea of being a woman of quality. What exactly is a woman of quality? A woman of quality is a woman who holds herself to high standards. She's responsible, reliable, and honest, as are the people closest to her. These women are resourceful, always evolving, and making their own lives better. Typically, they will hold the people in their lives to high standards as well because quality women don't tolerate being abused, mistreated, or being taken for granted. If you want to be with a quality man, you need to become a quality woman. You might already be a quality woman now. However, if you find yourself asking why you still haven't found your Mr. Right, you likely need to work on yourself. It's nothing to be ashamed of. We are all works in progress. And those around us serve as mirrors of that progress. This is what the law of attraction is all about. Take a moment and think about the type of qualities that you'd like in a man. Let's say that for the first thing you said you'd like in a man, you'd like one who works at a high paying job that he loves. Do you currently work at a high paying job that you love? A person who enjoys their work and makes more than enough money to fulfill their needs and their wants is vibrating energy differently than someone who hates their job and can't make ends meet.

Remember I said that we attract in our lives what we are. We do this energetically. If you haven't read the book *The Secret* by Rhonda Byrne or *Ask and It Is Given* by Esther Hicks, please do so as soon as possible. If I only had time to read one, I'd read the second as *The Secret* is more introductory regarding explaining the Law of Attraction. Also, it's a movie you can stream and watch on TV now. However, the book *Ask and It Is Given* is the most in-depth resource in the Universe on the topic of the law of attraction. All our thoughts emit an energetic frequency. Thoughts are things; this is now a proven scientific fact. Your thoughts create your energy body. If you're loving your job and making ends meet, surely, finding a man of this same caliber will be an easy task. If this isn't the case, maybe consider changing jobs? You can't attract something you aren't. Let's do another one. Pretend on your list of things you'd like in a man, you said, "I'd like someone with a good sense of humor." Do you have a good sense of humor? Do you laugh at funny things and make others laugh? Become that which you want in a man. Go through each item on your list and ask yourself, and preferably a close friend or family member, if you currently possess that same quality.

Another thing a quality woman knows how to do is to take care of herself and her needs, without needing a man to do so. If you leave yourself vulnerable in this way, you may end up accepting less than you desire. Don't leave any holes in your life. A hole in your life is any area that you feel incomplete or unfulfilled in. If you count on a man, or anyone else for that matter, to fill a hole, you will always count on them. Do you want to have to always be counting on someone else to make your life better and to make you feel complete? Women who do this are constantly finding themselves doing things they really don't want to be doing. It's a slippery slope too.

For example, let's say you're having a bad day, where everything just seems to be going wrong. You want to call up the guy you've been seeing for the past two weeks, but the relationship is still kind of new and you aren't sure if you should be calling him to discuss personal emotional matters. Ideally, in a good relationship, this is something you should be able to do. But do you want to always have to depend on him for that listening ear? If you don't have a girlfriend or family member to talk to, call a counselor or find a supportive community. In the big picture, the man you love, he will be there to listen to you and support you. However, before you've even determined your relationship status, it's not the right time to inundate your new guy with an inbox full of your problems. You will come off as being incredibly needy and possibly even a project yourself. Just imagine if you went out on a couple dates with this new guy and he seems to be simply perfect for you and you're really falling hard for him, and one day he calls you up on your lunch break, telling you how everything in his life is just such a mess and he is beside himself. Imagine that he even starts crying. Would you feel the same way about him as you did before the phone call? Or would you maybe begin to think that this guy doesn't really have his life together? The end game here is that it doesn't appear that this guy can take care of himself, right? So, how do you think it looks when you call a man blurting out your own emotional distress?

Human beings do need other human beings. We weren't made to function completely independently of one another. Let me make that clear right now. I'm not saying to never count on another person ever again. You shouldn't **have to** count on another person, but at times, we do need to count on one another. If you don't have many or any close friends, go out and make some. You do need to maintain other relationships outside of your life love. Your significant other should not be the only person you see and talk to on a day-to-day basis, at least not in a healthy relationship. Having friends or family members to talk to is essential. Please make sure that you have a loving network of supportive friends and family members available when you need to talk to someone. Guys you're casually dating are in your life for dating, not to be your personal psychotherapists. Spilling your problems to a guy you're out with is **not** something that a woman of quality does. If you find yourself doing this, please take a dating hiatus and get yourself together. Plug those holes. You have a hole in your emotional support network, and it **will** affect your love life until you repair it. Men don't care for drama, and they can sense when a woman doesn't value herself.

Self-evaluation and awareness are the most amazing tools you could ever utilize. Slowly go through each area of your life to determine how you feel regarding each area. Your feelings are there to guide you. Learn to trust them again. They won't ever lie to you. Which areas of your life would you like to improve? Asking yourself this question is the quickest way to find what's missing and correct the situation. We've already discussed your work and income areas of your life. What else makes you who you are? What kind of effort do you put into maintaining a nice home, clean car, or healthy body? Even more importantly than that, how do you nourish your mind and your soul? Mental and emotional health are no joke these days. Self-care and mental health are connected, and self-care needs to be your biggest priority, now and always! Thinking and feeling the wrong thoughts and feelings can cause a person to be very needy. How well do you care for you? You need to care about yourself and every aspect of your life. Go through each area of your life to see where you need to make any necessary changes. Fill any holes you find in your personal well-being. Remember, nothing changes until you do.

CHAPTER 7
ACTIONS AND BEHAVIORS

Only you know what you want and what you're willing to do to get it. If you were doing everything right, you would already have what you wanted by now. Obviously, your choices need some tweaking. And you can't change something about yourself if you're not aware that it's something that needs to be changed. Learning to toughen up will do wonders for you because you can't be overly sensitive about the things you're doing wrong. If you spend all your time feeling bad about the things you would like to change about yourself, how will you ever find the courage to make the necessary changes? You already know that there's things in your life that need changing. How honest with yourself can you be?

In the last chapter, we discussed filling the holes in your life. Now, we will need to go deeper. The choices you made yesterday have created the reality you're experiencing today. Our habits become us. It's in the small day to day things that we do that show us what's truly important to us. Each of us has our own unique strengths and weaknesses. Please be gentle with yourself when searching for ways you can better yourself. Have compassion for yourself because that's what people who love themselves do. They don't pity themselves, but they offer themselves grace. Don't beat up on yourself; I can't stress this enough! It does more harm than good, so please stop! Rise above your former self and find a higher vantage point to see where some positive changes can be made. If you can manage to keep your negative feelings out of it, it'll happen much quicker for you. Don't allow yourself to get emotional or have feelings about it. That will slow you down.

We are creatures of habit to such an extreme. Think about your habits. Are they good ones, moving you closer towards what you truly want, or could they use some improvement? How much time do you give yourself before having to be somewhere at a certain time? Do you leave yourself just enough time to get there or do you give yourself some extra time, so you can drive more relaxed and not have to worry if something comes up to delay you, such as a traffic jam? I used to be that person who would give myself just enough or not quite enough time to get wherever I had to go. Now, if I need to go somewhere that takes me 20 minutes to get there, I'll allow myself at least 40 minutes of travel time. That's just one good habit I've learned to develop. It's made my life run a ton more smoothly. Doing that has eliminated any anxiety I'd feel if I'd had to rush. What are some poor or self-defeating habits that you may have? Please don't say "none." If there were truly none, your life would be exactly as you'd like it to be, because you would've already been doing the things that you need to do to get what you want.

Another bad habit many people have is procrastination. Have you ever heard that saying, "Why put off until tomorrow what you can get done today?" Telling ourselves that conditions will be more favorable tomorrow is a tool for the unsure, afraid, or insecure. It's okay to not know what you need to do to get where you want exactly. The important thing is that you're taking action anyways. It's okay to get it wrong, but it's not okay to not try at all. You can fine tune your actions as time goes on. Just take some inspired action and I promise you that the Universe will step in and help, as long as you keep going. When we continuously tell ourselves "Tomorrow," we never get to experience what we want because all we have is now. Tomorrow never really comes. Leave procrastination in the past by taking ANY action, any small action at all. Don't be afraid. Dive in and tackle it head on and it'll change you for the better.

What other positive actions or behaviors can you establish right now to create a better future? In previous chapters, we talked about not blaming others and taking responsibility for our actions, but we didn't discuss much about complaining. Complaining is a terrible habit that keeps us stuck in victim mode. Whatever we resist persists. If you don't want it in your reality, you need to stop giving your attention to it. The Universe is always responding to our current energetic vibration. If you're stuck on what's missing from your life, all the Universe can do is give you more things to miss in your life. You choose what your focus is on in every single moment and the Universe is, in turn, responding to that focus. If you're feeling grateful for something, the Universe will give you more to be grateful for. Feeling gratitude puts you in direct alignment with source energy and everything that you've ever wanted. Constantly look for things to be grateful for and you'll be so much happier! The universal law of assumption states that we get in life is not what we want, but *who we are being* in any given moment (Identity). I find this law more relevant than the law of attraction and I am a certified law of attraction life coach. No matter how much we may want something, if receiving that thing doesn't feel natural, then we're not ready for it. This goes back to not putting things on pedestals. I incorporate both into my coaching. We attract WHO WE ARE BEING far more than what we want.

If you're complaining about something you don't like, your current focus is on lack, a lack of what you want. And by continuing to complain, you're reinforcing that lack, and asking the Universe to send you more things for you to complain about. Is that what you want? Think about the last time you complained about something. How did it make you feel? Generally speaking, no one feels joyous while complaining. You lower your energetic frequency when you decide to focus it on what you don't want, rather than on what you do want. We live in an abundant universe, and this means that if you're stuck in a lack mentality, the universe is sending you more things, people, circumstances, and events that recreate that very same feeling of lack! You're receiving an abundance of lack because you've tuned your radio (your energy, thoughts, and feelings) to a station that only plays lack. It's just as easy and way more fun to tune into that of abundance, an abundance of health, wealth, and love can take you far! Change the station!

To get out of the blame and complain game, you need to consciously choose to think and feel differently. Monitor your feelings as often as possible. Set alarms on your phone and check your mood. Shift your focus to what you do want. See these situations differently. Rather than complaining about paying your cell phone bill this month, be grateful that you have a cell phone that connects you with loved ones and that the company entrusted you enough to provide you with their services! There are people in the world who don't even have a phone. Those people would just love to be able to pay a cell phone bill. Start paying attention to your thought patterns and unconscious habits. Learn to evaluate your daily choices and grow from them. As you become aware of new desires within you, you'll have to grow and stretch yourself to attain these desires, so you will always be re-evaluating and reinventing yourself.

Gaining control of your emotions, especially after a lifetime of letting them run amok, isn't easy. It'll take a great commitment on your part. Your emotions don't run your life, you do. Emotional intelligence is something that can truly make or break you. Saying that you have no control over your own emotions is the lazy person's way out. Sure, it might feel that way sometimes and there definitely are moments in time when we do flip out or lose control or need to just take a day. Those times are the exception, not the rule. On a day-to-day basis, you should be able to control your emotions. They're meant to be felt briefly for guidance. Certain bad feelings can seem to last forever at times, but it's up to you not to let them control you. Feeling your emotions is the key to getting rid of them. Sit with difficult feelings and allow them to pass by soaking into them. Taking substances, drinking alcohol, overeating, or any other distraction you use to take your mind off the pain will only suppress it into your body where it can eventually manifest as an actual illness. Feelings are either felt, processed, and released or stored as energy that takes on a physical form within your body as disease. Please always allow yourself to feel your feelings and then let them go. Taking any form of substance just suppresses that feeling into your body—it's still there! Over time, this can build up in your system and make you physically sick, and I mean really sick.

One very important thing to remember about emotions is that they can convey weakness. If you constantly allow your emotions to control you and dictate your behavior, you will be perceived by others as weak-minded. We all experience incredibly difficult times in our lives, every single one of us. But it's in how we see our way through these difficult times that will define us and determine who we become. Your choices shape your character. You can choose to take control of your feelings or allow them to take control of you. One thing's for sure is that they will control you if you don't take control of them. Did you ever notice how differently people are treated when they speak in a calm and cool manner? They seem to be more respected and heard by others. Yet, how do people tend to react to people who are hysterical or screaming? Usually, the emotional person is viewed as the less stable one and often, not even heard by others. Please always acknowledge and feel your feelings. Just try not to swim in the negative ones. Your ESS (emotional sensing system) is meant to help navigate, not to sit stuck at one place for very long. It will always guide you to what you want.

If you'd really like to nail this whole self-improvement and empowerment thing, you will really need to learn to become a master of your emotions. If you're still concerned about your feelings being hurt, it'll be very challenging for you to hear the constructive criticism that is necessary before change can occur. Whether it's you yourself realizing where changes need to be made, or a close friend, you can't cry about it. Well, sometimes crying is necessary and can release stored trauma, so please cry when you feel the need to. Just don't cry when you ask for constructive criticism to help you better yourself. Listening with an open heart is the only way to realize what you need to change. Be a mature adult about it.

Also, this isn't a one-time endeavor. This is something you should be doing for the rest of your life. You should always be trying to be better and create more than you did yesterday. There will always be a need for you to re-evaluate yourself to see where you can make improvements. Once I was able to open myself to constructive criticism, I began to look for it. Of course, any changes I made within myself were filtered by me first, only if it was something I felt I wanted to improve within myself. You should never do something another person suggests without consulting with yourself first. Once I started changing the "bigger" things that I could change in my life, then I began to look for other smaller ways that I could improve my life.

Knowledge can come from any source too. Always be open to all forms of knowledge, learning, and information because you never know how it's going to come to you. The more open you are to trying new things, going to new places, and meeting new people, the faster you will grow. The biggest life lessons usually tend to involve other people. Learning more about yourself is the best way to make improvements in your life. Whether it's through reading, searching online, seeking out an expert, or spending time with others, or taking a class, we learn new things every single day. Relationships and how we relate to others is the main way we learn, through each other. Sometimes the biggest lessons we need to learn are the hardest to hear. Keep that in mind if you've met with some criticism that triggers you. Chances are that if someone has touched upon a sensitive topic with you and you're triggered by it, it's because you have unhealed aspects attached to the idea. Don't discard their words. Sometimes the more offended we feel by what a person says, the closer we need to look at what they're saying. It may be right on the money! Something inside of you was activated by something they said which means there's something inside of you that needs to be healed.

I like to make a game out of life sometimes. It's fun when you realize how truly powerful you are, to just sit back and watch things unfold. Watch others and how they talk and react, and even more importantly, watch yourself. At the end of each day, you should take a few minutes to evaluate your day and how you carried yourself. What could you have done better today that you will do better tomorrow? Did you say something that you wish you hadn't said, and how can you better use your words next time? Did you do the things you need to do today to make your tomorrow better? The biggest determining factor in how much good we receive in life is how thankful we are for what's in our lives now. If you're aware of all the good parts of your life and your focus is there, your energy is vibrating at a much faster rate. Love is the highest vibration!

People seem to have a difficult time stating things they're grateful for and the reason for this is because most of us take our blessings for granted. If I asked you to write a list of things you're grateful for and you write down, "I'm grateful for my home, my family, and my job," well you're not trying very hard and not really seeing a lot of the things in your life that you could be grateful for. The deeper you dig for things you appreciate, the deeper the Universe will dig in, finding you more things to be grateful for. There are a million books out there on the topic of gratitude. If you'd like to go deep with gratitude, feel free to check out the gratitude journal I've written, titled *An Advanced Gratitude Journal* which is available on Amazon. It goes deep into gratitude; into areas we don't often think about. Along with love and joy, I feel gratitude may be one of the strongest forces in the Universe. The quickest way to climb up the emotional scale and attract your desires is through gratitude and having a proper understanding of the law of attraction. The law of assumption is equally important if not more so. Please google the term "emotional scale" so you know what I am referring to. I have a copy of it inside the gratitude journal I've written for reference.

What are you appreciating right now? Appreciation with the Universe can be compared to a Lego tower. I am referring to those small blocks that children play with, that stick into one another to build things. Imagine piling one Lego on top of another, and another, and another. Now, imagine that each Lego represents one thing in your life that you are grateful for. When I say "things," I don't just mean material possessions. I am referring to anything you are grateful for, anything at all. It can be a person, a place, a thing, a feeling, a service, an experience, or an idea. It can literally be anything. See each Lego as one thing in your life that you both see (awareness) and appreciate (gratitude). Feel gratitude for these things now. Let's pretend you have ten things that you're grateful for right now, which means you have a Lego tower of ten Legos. Being fully aware of these Legos and this tower, the Universe is going to add ten more Legos! But, if you don't see all the Legos you have right now, what is your tower made from? You can't build a tower without any materials. How can the Universe add to it when you aren't even aware of its existence or you never built it? The Universe will match you. Start to actively seek out things to appreciate. In your spare time, or when waiting in a line, look around you and take in your surroundings. Be aware of what's around and think about what you appreciate. This changes your vibration which then changes the things you become a match for. When you vibrate in gratitude and love, your energy level is higher, and you now have access to better feeling emotions. Life will begin bringing you people, events, and circumstances that match your new higher energy level. People and things who you are no longer a match with will just "fall away." In the book *Ask and It is Given* by Abraham or Esther Hicks, she has a process in the back of the book that she calls, "The Placemat Process." It first occurred to her while at lunch with her husband Jerry. She was feeling overwhelmed by all the things that she had to do so she decided to use the placemat in the restaurant and draw a line down in the center. One side was titled, "things I can do myself," and the other side was titled, "things I'm handing over to the universe." Every single thing she released and let the universe take care of was completed! We really do have unseen help if we can learn to just trust and believe in it!

Think about people who can only wish to be doing the things that you take for granted. We tend to only notice how important things are once they're gone, like electricity and our health. How much do you miss electricity when you don't have any for hours at a time, or even worse, days? During a wicked storm that occurred where I live, everyone lost power. And it wasn't for a day or two, it was for several weeks. We were in a state of emergency, which happens somewhat frequently here. Things like that really teach you to appreciate all that you have that you tend to take for granted. We all do it to some degree. You could come up with a list of a million things you're grateful for if you really tried. The thing is, if you can't think of it, you're not currently appreciating it!

Complaining is the quickest way to lower your vibration and attract negativity to yourself. Choose to see what IS there, rather than what isn't. It's like being inside the solution, rather than staying stuck inside the problem. The law of attraction can only match your vibration. It will never give you something you aren't asking for with your thoughts and feelings.

The law of attraction is just like the law of gravity. It exists and is playing a role in your life. Whether you believe in it or not, it's still happening. Your options are to either master it and make your life great or ignore it and continue to leave your life up to chance. Personally, I love having the power in my own hands to change my life for the better. You can say you don't believe in gravity but go and try to step off the roof of a tall building and tell me what happens. If you say that you don't believe in the law of attraction, you're doing yourself a great injustice because it's far better to be armed with the knowledge, than to be simply floating along wondering why things aren't better for you. The sooner you learn about the law of attraction, the sooner you can begin to change your life. Just because you don't know it's working behind the scenes, doesn't make it any less real. It's always working in your life on your behalf. Don't you think it's a good idea to know what it's all about?

The law of attraction states that like attracts like. All creation begins with a thought. Think about what you desire and you're giving it energy, just by thinking about it. Everything is energy. Before anything can manifest in your physical reality, it begins inside you, as a thought. Thoughts are things. Thoughts have energy. Thoughts are what creates your life. The Universe doesn't have a moral compass. It only reads energy. If you're worrying about something, you're vibrating much slower and attracting whatever you're worrying about to show up in your life. Negative thinking and anxiety rob you of your dream life. Worrying is telling the universe to send you exactly what you don't want! It's so debilitating. You could be spending that time feeling and envisioning an amazing life for yourself instead! Think BIGGER. If you struggle to make the law of attraction work for you in your life, look to the law of assumption. It all goes back to your identity or who you are at your core! I feel the two universal laws work together because the law of assumption states that we "attract what we are," not necessarily "what we want." For example, let's say you'd like to attract a loving relationship into your life, but your core identity tells you that you're not good enough or not healed enough for love, then, that's what you will attract. You'll attract someone else who feels not good enough about himself or no one at all. You always have to feel deserving of the things you want, or you simply won't manifest them. Can you see how these two laws work together?

On the other hand, having faith that things are working out for you and thinking positively will raise your vibration. Always look for things you like and that make you feel good. Escape negative feelings as soon as possible. Your beliefs play a big part here too because the only things that aren't possible for you are those that you believe aren't possible. All things are created on the inside, before they can manifest on the outside. Everything you see around you was once a thought someone had. The life you are living now is a result of your past thoughts. Furthermore, the life you live a year from now will be based on the way you think right now. Think good thoughts. Believe in endless possibilities for yourself. When you don't believe you can get what you want in life, you create resistance. The biggest manifestation blocker is resistance. The law of attraction is always going to match your current vibration. If you're feeling bad or sad, the Universe will bring you more things to feel sad or bad about. But if you're feeling good and grateful, the Universe will bring you more things to be grateful for and good about. You tune yourself like a radio to a higher frequency or a different station, and that's just the beginning. Once there, you will experience new things you couldn't experience before at the lowered frequency you previously existed at. New adventures await you. From there, you'll birth more new desires that are more in alignment with the new you. Have a happy attitude no matter what circumstances you're in.

I mentioned that the law of attraction begins with a thought. The real magic is in the feeling that comes with the thought. Our thoughts create our feelings. Our feelings are repeated and have energized thoughts attached to them. When you feel good, you're at an elevated vibration and feeling bad lowers your vibration. One negative experience won't drastically lower your vibration unless you choose to dwell on it and have a negative attitude about it. This is where emotional intelligence comes to your rescue. Shake it off. You aren't a victim unless you decide to be one. That means that when something bad does happen, it's up to you to choose how you want to deal with it. People who are more positive and happier seem to have an easier time letting things go. Or even just starting off being positive and staying that way all day by practicing moments of gratitude for small things, like no waiting in line. Forget about blaming and take responsibility. If it's within your power to choose, it's also within your power to change!

Learning about the law of attraction is by far, the single smartest decision I've ever made. It's helped my life more than any of my college degrees, money, friends, or experiences ever could. Knowing my true range of possibilities is priceless. And this power (or ability to see possibilities where you once saw lack), you have it too. You have it now. Maybe you just aren't aware of it or how to use it to your fullest advantage. If knowledge is power, knowing the law of attraction is one of the most formidable weapons you could have in your lifetime. If you are interested in the law of attraction and it's new to you, please see the movie *The Secret* with Rhonda Byrne. It's also a book, but the movie has some great interviews in it. Also, Esther Hicks is quite a well-known expert in this field and has several books and a full video series on it. If you enjoy having the power to create your best life possible, these resources will surely help you get there. Read them repeatedly too, because as you change, your understanding of the material also changes. Another amazing resource, and my favorite book in the world is by Neville Goddard, titled, *The Power of Imagination*. It combines a bunch of his books into one and focuses on the law of assumption. He even breaks down parts of the Bible to describe what the TRUE meanings are, rather than the literal meanings that people assume to be true. I highly recommend this book!

Just think back to how many times you read a book or saw a movie a second time and you got something new out of it. Growth and change occur in a spiral. We go back to things from our past for a further or deeper understanding. You go back to get sprung ahead. That's how it works. Nothing is linear, not even time. If you're trying to make a lot of positive changes in your life, and you know you're doing your best, and yet, some negative things still tend to happen, please know that this is just to propel you forward. It's only temporary. Life is always happening FOR YOU and THROUGH YOU but is never happening "to you," which is how most of us see it. Please don't get caught up in the negativity of the moment. Know that this is happening for your highest good. Did you ever notice how right before things in your life get really good, they tend to completely fall apart? Again, it's the spiral. Just look back at your life, at times that were wonderful. Did it happen shortly after your life fell apart? You can't build anew until you tear down the old, right? It seems like common sense.

Many people think it's so much easier to look outside of ourselves for the answers, but that's not the case at all. We've been so programmed away from our own power that we've forgotten its existence altogether! This has made us scared and out of practice. There's so much that we've forgotten or lost along the way that we need to get back. It would seem easier to believe in a powerful force outside of us. I enjoy counting on myself for almost everything. Asking someone else for answers to your life problems isn't always the way to go. What is important to you may not be important to the person you're relying on for sound advice. I do hope that you have a supportive network of family and friends there for you, because that does help a lot on bad days. However, if you don't, no worries. There's absolutely nothing wrong with being your own best friend. Believing in yourself and your abilities is necessary. At certain times in life, we all need to count on someone else. Recent research studies are finally showing that the most intelligent people prefer to spend time alone. But community is important and people who are a part of a supportive community have been scientifically proven to live longer and happier lives. So don't beat up on yourself if you're going through a period of isolation. Just be sure to get back out there when you're feeling up to it. Life is all about relationships with other people, places, and things. We experience ourselves through our relationships. We're all mirrors for one another.

If you were the ultimate power, or had ultimate power, would you continue to search outside of yourself for answers? This is the point that I'm trying to make. I need you to learn to count on yourself for things that you hadn't been previously. Be responsible for your own actions and choices because you can't take your mom or your best friend with you everywhere. Allowing another person to make major life decisions for you weakens your core. Trial and error are your best teachers. Someday you could find yourself in a position where the only person you can count on for help or answers is yourself. What will you do in this situation if it were to occur? Would you throw your hands up in the air and give up, or take on the challenge with an open mind? While it's great to have friends and even necessary, you shouldn't count on them like a lifeline. You must learn to care for yourself and be there for yourself. Strength is sexy too. **Men love women who are soft on the outside but tough as nails on the inside!**

Another reason to be aware of this powerful force inside of you is to know that you are always supported and cared for. The Universe adores you! You're never alone either, as long as you don't abandon yourself. You can learn to count on your own higher power within yourself for every single answer you could ever want. You have infinite wisdom inside of you. We all do. All you need is to simply tap into that power. You can't tap into it if you don't even believe it exists. Begin to cultivate a relationship with this higher power you have within yourself. Deep down, you've always known it's there and always felt its presence. Now, you need to acknowledge it on a more significant level. Learn your true abilities because, I promise you, there is nothing you can't be, do, or have. It all lies within your belief and faith in yourself.

CHAPTER 8
SO VERY IN LOVE WITH ME

If you don't like or love yourself, why should anyone else? We can control ourselves, but we can't control other people. As long as you "need" or feel "attached" to any other human being, they will always have some type of power over you. The only way to be fully free is to disconnect from all other living things and have no attachments. The purest love is unattached. When you don't need anyone for anything at all, that's when you can learn to be truly free. If you need someone, they control you. Nobody controls a Goddess.

If you truly love yourself, this isn't asking a lot of you. Those of you who are mentally whining right now, you're the ones who need this the most. Learn to be your own best friend because the only person who will be along for the entire journey with you is you. Why not discover who you are, get to know yourself, and fall madly in love with yourself? Because society says we should neglect ourselves and be there for others? Oh wait, does society pay my bills? Nope. Scrap that one then!

Right now, some part of you might not agree with all of this, but I promise you it works. It makes everything better. Spending time with yourself means that you're making yourself a priority. It's not about who you could be spending your time with or what you could be doing. It's about cultivating the person you would like to become. You should enjoy the time you spend alone, learning about what you like and enjoy doing. Who do you trust more than yourself? If you don't like being alone, please ask yourself why. Nothing in your life is more important than you liking and loving yourself. If your core isn't solid, anyone or anything can take you over. Strength is a necessity and being able to stand on your own two feet is gigantic in terms of self-growth. Spending time by yourself also helps you get to know yourself. Many of us are people-pleasers and aren't even aware of the fact that we don't know ourselves because we've spent so much time pleasing other people! Please spend some quiet time alone getting to know yourself. You won't feel like you constantly need to be around other people then either. And don't distract yourself with mindless scrolling on social media or other types of screen time. Pick up a book or take a walk in nature. Turn on "Do Not Disturb" on your phone and refrain from looking at it.

When you're not with other people, you don't need to consider their feelings or opinions and there's a beautiful freedom in that. The only person you need to be concerned with is yourself. You get to know yourself much better. And if you happen to be a people pleaser, which is how many of us start out, you can take a break from that. The only person I want you to please right now is yourself. Please make yourself a priority. In this society, we all have been brainwashed with the ludicrous idea that it's wrong to love ourselves or put ourselves first. What a joke! Who came up with that garbage? The first person you should be concerned with is yourself. If you spend all your time with other people, how are you honoring yourself and your soul? How well do you know yourself? How do you know that the decisions you make are what YOU want, versus what your company wants? When you're with other people, unless you magically agree on everything, compromises need to be made. One person will have to sacrifice what they want for what the other person wants. Ideally, friendships should be even and equal and you take turns choosing activities. This isn't always the case though.

One thing that I want you to keep in mind through all of this is that you always have your friends. And if you don't have any friends, you have yourself, if you haven't abandoned yourself. If so, please come back into your body now and embody that body! I say it because I've lived it! When you're constantly focused on other people or feeling sad that no one has contacted you, you've left yourself! Focusing on yourself and being present brings you back into your body! Being alone doesn't mean all alone. In this scenario, it simply means being without a significant other. You can spend time with friends. One thing that I've learned the hard way is that many women would rather spend all their free time with their man. So, if you think that your female friends will be available for frequent socialization, don't count on it! Smart women don't revolve their lives around men or ditch their friends for some random guy they barely know. NEVER ditch a friend for a man. I can't begin to tell you how many different friends of mine have told me how certain friends or family members of theirs will vanish as soon as they meet a new guy. Then as soon as the new guy realizes this woman would never mentally stimulate him or be any type of a challenge, he dumps her! Can you guess what this woman does next? Yep, she calls the female friend that she initially ditched to be with this jerk! Sad but true, too many women don't know how to be alone.

While I'm on this topic, I need to mention something additional, about having guys for friends. There's been an ongoing dispute about whether men and women can be friends. Men and women can be friends if they both make an agreement in advance and put in the effort to follow through. If you're following the information provided in this book correctly, chances are that most men you meet won't be seeing you as a potential friend. They're going to want more from you. What do you do in a situation like this? You stick to your guns. You don't "feel bad" for the guy and give yourself to him. You not wanting them, it just makes you that much more appealing! Know what you want and make a conscious decision to stop at nothing to get it. Many people believe that men and women absolutely can't be friends. I think this is 90 percent true only because one of the two, if not both, tend to develop feelings for the other. Sometimes the guy just starts to feel attracted to the woman sexually and tries for that. Each situation is unique, but forearmed is forewarned about having men for friends. Being friends with men comes with great benefits! They can teach you about how men think and how men are and vice versa. If you decide to be more than friends, just make sure you're both equally healed and mentally and emotionally healthy. Best friends usually have the happiest marriages. Please don't look for this from the start though. Enjoy the friendship for what it is.

What do you do on a lonely night at home when your ex calls you to come over? You know you don't need to make a commitment right, so what's there to lose? The answer will surprise you. You have a lot to lose. You never know what "emotional place" you will be in upon leaving there. Also, you don't know what emotions or attachments will be stirred up while you're there. In the song by Dua Lipa, titled *New Rules*, she sings, "If you're under him, you're not getting over him!" Many women are easily swayed or manipulated by men. We let our emotions take over and believe what we want to believe to make the situation what we want it to be. When we give our bodies away, we're also giving away our power. Notice how different men can be after they've had sex with you. Never be a booty call, not ever, not for anyone! Don't even let him swing by your place. This keeps you in a lower frequency and matches you to lower quality men.

Once you can be happy alone, you can do anything! You stop needing other people for things. Choosing for yourself becomes easier. You become like a massively strong rock that can weather any storm. When you fill yourself, you don't need other people to make you happy anymore. You make yourself happy. Other people are great for socializing, but you learn to stop counting on them for your happiness. It's never a good idea to base your happiness on anything outside of yourself. The only person, place, or thing that can make you truly happy, is you. Happiness is simply a choice, nothing more, nothing less. You can choose to be happy right now, no matter how awful you think your life might be. *Find the good in it.* Every good feeling we experience in life comes from inside of us. Read that again about ten times because it's that important! If you're able to read this right now, that means that you either have a cell phone or computer access, so, it's not likely that you're homeless. Count your blessings. That's the quickest way to improve your life. The Universe is not going to hand you more if you haven't even acknowledged what you've already got. Start there. Always fulfill your own needs, in every area of life. Again, no man is an island unto himself, and we do need others. Please note that. However, you should be self-sufficient as much as possible, and not *need* to solely rely on anyone else for your own happiness.

There are so many reasons why you should make it a practice to spend some time alone. During my alone time, I've made the most progress in my life. I always try to utilize it to my advantage because time is our most valuable commodity. Don't squander it. Start valuing your time. Pay attention to how you feel while with certain people and when you leave certain people. If you feel drained during or after, it may be time for some new people. Good friends should leave you feeling fulfilled afterwards, or what's the point? Just like when you're a good date and you end the date early, you leave the man wanting more of you! Seriously consider where you spend your time, who you spend it with, and how it makes you feel. You can make more money, but you can never make more time. We have so much and that's it. People need to stop and reflect. Otherwise, we're on a treadmill, simply repeating the same day over and over like the movie *Groundhog Day*. If you never stop and contemplate, nothing changes.

You don't have to go through months of your life being alone like a new nun in the convent. But you should set aside time for yourself every day to evaluate and explore your own life and desires. It's all about doing you, and currently, it seems far more difficult to find time for that. Don't always jump at an offer to go out, whether it's for fun for yourself or to help another out, especially if you need to do something for yourself at home or have other plans. If you had plans to go to yoga, for a walk, or to a class, and you blow it off to socialize, who are you hurting? You only hurt yourself. Of course, there are times to work and times to play. A lot of this is about balance. You need to learn to balance your time and energy and put more faith and time into yourself than you do into others. Delegate your time as you see fit and modify it as needed. To stay strong, you do need to make time for yourself every day. Whether it's exercising, meditating, or journaling, just do it. It's a promise to yourself for a better life. I highly recommend all three of those activities, especially the journaling. I have my own gratitude journal, and I know why so many people talk about the positive benefits of gratitude. Gratitude is magic. No joke. Start each morning writing a few things you're grateful for and why. The more you can see, the more the universe will give you to experience. The why is the most important part, it's the feeling part. Feel appreciative for everything, and everything will be yours. Find a way to incorporate "me time" into every single day of your life. Shoot for at least an hour. Your life should feel complete without anyone else in it. Now begins the fun part of choosing what you will do with your time. Our habits become us, as do our thoughts and feelings. The feeling is the REAL secret in all of this regarding creation.

CHAPTER 9
HELLO GODDESS!

There's just something so appealing about a woman of character and strength. She's not someone to trifle with and usually her energy enters a room even before she does. You can't take her over. You can't control her and you sure as hell can't manipulate her. And it's not about her appearance, although, her inner beauty always makes her outer beauty shine. It's in her everything. Surely, you have someone like this in your life that you can relate to. These women who seem to have it so good, that at times, you may have even wished you were them. This book will give you every single tool you need to become that woman and realize and embrace the Goddess residing within. You're already a Goddess, you just haven't fully realized it yet!

For those of you who have been wondering where the tips are to unleash your inner love goddess, you've arrived. Although, I must tell you that most of what is attractive to others comes from the inside out. Attraction is an inside job. Ninety-five percent of the changes I've made within myself, were on the inside. Everything is about the inside. All the things you see on the outside started on the inside. First, we manifest what we desire on the inside. Once we bring ourselves into alignment with what we want by matching our energy to that thing, by knowing it's ours for the taking, feeling and releasing it, then, and only then, will you experience it in your outer world. Expectation is the key to getting what you want! True beauty is also an inside job too. A woman who is beautiful on the outside, but is cruel to others, soon becomes unattractive on the outside as well. The inside and the outside cannot be truly separated. Attitude is everything! Appearances will only get you so far.

A Goddess knows who she is and loves who she is. Goddesses are secure in knowing who they are and what they want from life, and they make it happen. My favorite Goddess is Cleopatra. I will be using her as an example often throughout this chapter because she is my personal favorite. She was romanced by leaders like Julius Caesar and Mark Antony, and she took down entire cities with her charm! Cleopatra was well known all over the world for her beauty, but it was actually her intelligence that won her a place in history. Also, if you check the history books, you will find that the real Cleopatra didn't quite look as beautiful as she has been portrayed throughout history by such gorgeous women as Elizabeth Taylor. In reality, Cleopatra wasn't a perfect 10. She considered herself to be masculine and didn't much care for her nose. Nonetheless, she didn't let any of that stand in her way. A true goddess accepts who she is, embracing any perceived flaws, loves what she looks like, loves who she is, and uses it all to her advantage. They say it was her voice and her charm that won men over. I think she was an incredibly strong woman, who had been through more than one could ever imagine, and she embraced her identity. Goddesses do that. They go through hardships, often. Pain can and does contribute to beauty if you allow yourself to grow from it, rather than become a victim of it.

More importantly though, is that goddesses know how to put themselves first. They make themselves a priority. Today, we're all worried about being there for others and neglecting ourselves and wondering why things are the way they are. Cleopatra did what she had to do, to get where she needed to be in life. If it just so happened that it meant killing her brother, she was up for that task too. Not once, but twice. She killed both of her brothers and a sister as well, to thwart off rivals to the throne of Egypt. Now, I am not suggesting that you go and kill your siblings, even if they do have it coming. But there's a lesson to be learned here.

You don't mess with a goddess. A goddesses' priority is always herself. True goddesses never need to learn how to go about finding a man because fending them off truly is something that goddesses contend with daily. It doesn't matter if you never had a man chase you a single day in your life before now. If you follow, understand, and implement everything I've outlined here in these pages, you will embrace the Goddess within and chasing off men will become your reality. I can't say that you will "become" a goddess, because I know that you already are one. It's time now that you knew it too.

As a goddess, there are certain things you must understand. You no longer go out of your way for men, or anyone really. Those days are over. Let them please you. And believe me, they will. Men live to please us. It's true. Go and ask a guy if he'd rather be with a doormat that kisses his ass or a goddess who won't give him the time of day. Seems like a no-brainer, doesn't it? People in general enjoy a challenge. Not just men. I hear so many women talking about guys needing and wanting a challenge, and women act annoyed by this. Ladies, you're no different, and you know this. We like the adventure, excitement, and thrill just as much as the guys do, don't we? Or are you secretly pining away for your stalker behind closed doors? I didn't think so. The less you do for a man, the more valuable he will begin to see you. Women who are labeled as "high maintenance" are those women who do put themselves first, know what they want, and are not willing to compromise. If you're not valuing yourself, you're going to end up with a man who doesn't value himself or you. Listen to some Aretha Franklin and learn to respect yourself. If you don't value you, why would someone else value you? If you don't like who you are, why should anyone else? Out of sympathy, or out of pity? No thanks. That's not what you want is it, for people to feel sorry for you? Don't be a charity case.

Before I continue, I need to interject with a few words about self-insults. It's the most unattractive characteristic a person can ever display. It's like holding a billboard sign over your head that says, "I don't like myself and I want to make sure that you know it." Even insulting your past self is detrimental because time isn't linear.

You hold yourself in such a negative vibrational pattern when you continue to put yourself down. Just imagine you're out on a date with what you consider to be a classy guy and in the middle of the conversation he says something like, "I love your outfit, mine is too tight, I need to lose some weight." Granted, you generally don't hear guys talking like that, but how would you feel if you did experience that? While you might not be able to put your feelings into words in that moment, you would be instantly struck with the impression that this guy doesn't much like himself. Now, unless you also dislike yourself, this would be an instant turn-off to a person and a red flag! So, next time you're on a date or around a guy you like, keep the self-criticism to yourself. Definitely don't fish for compliments either. That's being insecure and not what a Goddess is.

I advise you against ever putting yourself down, but especially don't do it around someone you're interested in. Stating things that you dislike about yourself is a sure way to attract someone who dislikes themselves as well and these people will start seeing you in the same way that you see yourself. And remember your frequency too. Do you think that people who live from love and gratitude would ever vibrate from a place of self-insults? Whether it's from the past or about the past, it doesn't matter. Your subconscious knows just you and just this moment. The only moment that ever exists is now. Did you want to plant a seed of negativity on your own behalf into the garden of your subconscious mind? I didn't think so.

When I stopped going out of my way for men, it was quite interesting. I'd make requests, without expectations. I'd tell them what I wanted, whilst not expecting anything from them, but full well knowing the entire time that it wasn't something I was about to do for myself. If a guy is worthy, he will jump at an opportunity to please you. No request is too big or too small either. When a woman is constantly doing things for a man, he gets bored quickly. It doesn't take long for a man to realize when a woman doesn't value herself. Any woman who jumps through hoops for a man, surely doesn't value or love herself. A woman without any self-respect is a turn-off to men. Men love to be excited and confused at the same time when it comes to dating, sex, and love. They don't want a sure thing. They like mystery and adventure. A man never knows what to expect from a goddess. She knows exactly how to keep her man on his toes. He's always searching for new ways to please her. If a man tries to please you, and you aren't impressed, say so. This is not the time to care about his feelings or placate his emotions. This is the time to let him know you won't settle. If you said you wanted a filet mignon and he brings home chuck steak, reiterate that your request was for filet mignon. He may act annoyed and not want to go back and exchange it, but you showed him that you expect the best. In the future, it's highly unlikely that he will be bringing chuck steak home again. Goddesses are full of desires. Continue to raise the bar. Always make him work for it. Julius Caesar erected a gilded statue of Cleopatra in the temple of Venus Genetrix. What have you inspired a man to do lately?

The first step towards embracing the goddess within is to make yourself feel like a goddess. Again, I am going to use Cleopatra for an example here. Can you picture her now? When you do picture her, what do you see in your mind's eye? I see a beautiful, dark-haired woman, adorned in gold, jewels, a golden crown, and stunning make up! Cleopatra was a goddess and a natural seductress. Women who are natural seductresses don't have to do much to capture a man's attention, but they thoroughly enjoy the entire beautification process from start to finish. How do you look when you leave the house each day? Do you make it a point to take care of yourself and your appearance? Or do you throw on any old thing, and run out the door in your pajamas? True goddesses enjoy their own beauty and love to play it up and bring out their best features. They know how to use everything to their advantage, and they don't care what others think of them. Their beauty is for their enjoyment alone. Now, this isn't about being superficial or shallow. It's about feeling good, by looking good. Goddesses have fun with this and enjoy it. Do you enjoy choosing your clothing, doing your hair, and makeup? Do you experiment with new colors, new hairstyles, and new makeup? Or maybe you dread this step. Don't. Enjoy all of it. Choose clothing that makes you feel good. What do your fingernails and toenails look like? Are they painted up all pretty or is it hammer time? Every single part of self-care shows the world how you feel about yourself and who you are and has everything to do with the type of men you will attract. Would you like to attract a man who looks like he just fell out of bed smelling like farts this morning or a man who took the time to get ready and obviously cares about his appearance? Again, we attract what we are. If you want a classy guy, you need to be a classy gal. Yes, it's that simple. And remember, you didn't sign a contract that said you had to be the same person that you were yesterday. You can wake up tomorrow and choose to be whoever and whatever you like. Go out and get yourself a whole new wardrobe. Make that appointment for a massage and eyebrow waxing. Cut and dye that hair if you want! If it makes you feel good, it's more than worth it. I know when I look good, I feel good too. Be a new you!

Some women will put themselves through hell to look appealing on the outside but do no inner work on themselves. Beauty shouldn't be uncomfortable. If squeezing into those jeans that are two sizes too small is your idea of what beauty is, you need to revamp your definition. There is a way to feel good, look good, and be comfortable in your own skin. If looking good is causing you physical pain, you're defeating the entire purpose. Nothing is more important than feeling good in the moment, and you couldn't possibly feel good by stuffing yourself into those tiny jeans to make a good impression. A good impression comes from who you are, not what you're wearing. I think it's safe to say that you will be far more relaxed when you're comfortable. Look beautiful and feel comfortable!

What is your daily beauty routine? Do you feel beautiful when you leave the house each day? You should, and if you don't, please work on that now. You should love your wardrobe, your shoes, your hair color, your hairstyle, your nails, your face and all that is YOU! If you don't, it's time to make some changes. This doesn't need to cost a fortune either. If money is tight, try a thrift shop for some new clothing or jewelry. Ask friends if they have any clothes they were thinking of donating. Tell them you're doing some inner work on yourself and that includes a makeover. Some may even want to join you! Maybe do a clothing swap. When was the last time you bought yourself a new purse or shoes that you just loved? What else can you do on the outside to feel great on the inside? While material possessions may not provide true or lasting happiness, if you enjoy and appreciate your new personal care items, they will benefit you in many future ways. When you're grateful for something, you will receive more of it.

If you currently find flaws in yourself for sport, you need to quit that right now. Please stop hurting yourself! You do yourself no good at all to not accept or love yourself. You hurt yourself and you also hurt all those you could have been helping by not embracing your true goddess within. That's the real you in there, not weighed down by society's ethics or the fear boxes you've placed yourself inside of. In chapter one, I spoke about being real with yourself. Please be real with others as well. Don't be afraid of what others think. I promise you that most people you encounter each day are far more concerned with what you think of them. When you realize who you really are, what you really want from life, I can assure you, you won't have any problems with being respected. Once you truly stop caring about what others think, you become invincible. As much as someone may want to knock you down from your high horse, you live up there, and it's simply not possible. Not when it's real and comes from within. You become completely fearless in just about every possible way. All goddesses have amazing lives that they've created by their own design, down to the tiniest of details. No, they aren't control freaks, but they really don't need others. Not in the sense that most people do. A goddess creates her life around herself and her desires. Have you created every aspect of your life? You sure did. You may not be consciously aware of that fact, but you have. And you do have the power to change any part of it that displeases you. The catch is, you're the only one who can.

What inner work do you do on yourself each day? Inner work is anything relating to changing you on the inside, not the outside. Only you can choose this for yourself because only you know what you genuinely want. Most of the time we aren't living in the moment and we're not even aware of it. Any time you're thinking about something other than what you're currently doing, you're not in the moment. You've removed yourself from time.

You've literally left yourself and the moment! You checked out, abandoned yourself! Be present! Presence is incredibly attractive!

I talk about that stream of well-being and abundance that the Universe is always flowing to us, and you need to know that it flows the best when it's not blocked by your thoughts. Our thoughts can either hinder or help us. If you can clear your mind for just a few minutes a day to start, it'll do wonders for you. Meditation is about observing your thoughts, not eliminating them. In time, you will think less and likely receive guidance from higher sources during your meditation practice. It's incredibly rewarding and can even heal your body! Exercise is for feeling good too. Get your heart pumping because that strengthens your cardiovascular system, which in turn lowers your heart rate and about a zillion other beneficial things, including the release of some fun hormones!

If you only have time for one of the three inner work exercises (meditation, exercise, gratitude), please choose gratitude. The Universe matches your gratitude. When you're in a state of gratitude, you're in total alignment with source energy and in receiving mode for the universe to bring you more things like those that you're already grateful for. Being aware of the blessings in your life is the quickest way to receive more blessings. Think back to the set of children's Lego blocks to better understand this concept. I explained this to my coaching groups a lot and it helped them conceptualize this idea. Each thing that you RECOGNIZE your appreciation for, it becomes a Lego. So, let's say that you stated and *feel* appreciation for living in a warm home, with all the comforts you could ever need. Now you have one visual Lego set up. Think of something else you truly appreciate. This will be Lego number two. The universe will build upon your Legos of gratitude, but if you don't put them there for the Universe to see by acknowledging them with **feelings** of appreciation, you won't get any more. But, if you continue to exercise the *feeling of gratitude* in your day-to-day life, the Universe will keep throwing more Legos up there so you can continue to appreciate more new things. While those Legos are always there, if you don't see them, it won't matter. The Universe sees what you see and feels what you feel.

I usually recommend that my clients keep a gratitude journal and write in it daily. List as many things as you possibly can that you are currently appreciating right now. Each item that you become aware of can take on a physical representation in your mind of that of a Lego and the Universe will see what you are building, and will always, always lend a hand. Adding the "why" to each item you're grateful for makes this practice ten times more beneficial because the "why" is the feeling behind gratitude and feelings are far more powerful than thoughts or words alone! Think quality over quantity. I used to list 25 things a day I was grateful for. Now I list like three to five and include the "why" for each item. That makes it far more powerful!

Of course, there are other ways you can work on yourself from the inside out, but these are my personal three favorites that don't take much time and pack quite a punch! Create a routine for yourself where you take a little time each day to work on yourself. Honestly, one hour a day is all it takes. Take care of your body and mind and they will take care of you right back. Choose a time of day that you won't be likely to have any distractions and make time for yourself. Turn off your phone ringer during this sacred time. This should be a daily habit, or part of your routine, if you want it to truly work for you. Rome wasn't built in a day, not even for Cleopatra, so be gentle with yourself. We're always our own worst critics, unfortunately. Self-compassion is a crucial part of loving yourself.

Now that you're ready to embrace the goddess within, let's have some fun with this! Are you ready to talk about dating and men? I bet you are after eight chapters discussing positive changes you need to make within yourself. Want to know where to meet men? The answer is simple, everywhere and anywhere! Personally, I like meeting someone in person. Words never seem to do a guy justice. They just don't. Online dating isn't the same as meeting someone face-to-face out there in the world. If that sounds scary to you right now, or even impossible, that's okay. Stick with the online thing that works for you for now. I've done that before too. However, in time, you will need to get out there. Confidence doesn't come from looking at a screen. It comes from practicing in the real world. Where in the real world can you meet men? Again, absolutely anywhere! If you're out and about in the world, guys will notice you and will hit on you. Even if this has never happened to you before, plan on it happening now! If you follow everything outlined above, you will have men flirting with you and wanting to take you out. It's just inevitable. One last word of advice here, unless you love to drink and are looking for a man who also loves to drink, don't look for men at a bar. I know I've repeated myself several times about this but it's just that important! Most of these men are just trying to get laid and aren't selective at all. I'm an incredibly spiritual person so I'd go to a meditation or spiritual place to meet men. What do you love to do? If you're stuck, go volunteer somewhere you consider to be a worthy cause. Whatever it is, go there, and go with the intention of participating in the activity and not specifically to meet men. Keep attending places like this that you love, doing things that you love, and in time you'll likely meet a man who you'll enjoy dating!

If you do all the inner work and it doesn't happen for you right away, try to take a step outside of yourself to see where you may be putting out a "lower vibe." Simply just having a bad day can seriously make a person unappealing if they're wearing it like clothing. Learn to shake it off and let it go and keep your vibration high. Energy is contagious and what we focus on expands. When you love yourself, others have no choice but to love you as well. If you don't know where to start or don't have many available friends for social activities, try Meetup.com or Alignable.com, or other local groups. You get to do what you love, while meeting new people, who also enjoy what you love. Sounds like a win-win to me! Of course, this isn't your only option, but it is one of them. You can meet men anywhere. If you love yourself and make all this really a part of you, it will become as natural as breathing. You're only limited in your own beliefs of what you think is possible for you.

Social media and dating sites or apps are other ways to meet men. There're millions of potential dating possibilities for you.

Make sure you know what your dealbreakers are with men and don't settle, so be sure to ask a ton of questions. Try not to drag out chatting for a long time because people can appear to be anyone they want through a screen, but only in person do you really know whether you two are compatible or not. Try to have phone calls and face time with the guy first to be sure you aren't wasting your time. Anyone can say anything in a text message, and you can't feel or express feelings this way. Do you feel better when someone actually smiles at you in person or sends you a smile emoji? Point made. If you eventually decide to meet up for a date, please be careful and let another person who knows you and cares about you know where you're going and who you're going with, just to be safe. I highly recommend driving your own car so you can leave early if you need to. Don't tolerate any type of disrespect or mistreatment. If the guy asked you out on the date, he should be paying for everything, including the tip. You're a goddess and goddesses don't pay for themselves. And go home alone that night! You have no clue who this guy is or what he's packing in his pants and no, I don't mean his size! The sooner you meet in person, the sooner you can decide if he's someone worth seeing again or if he's not for you. You can waste months chatting with someone online who is all wrong for you. Many of these guys are usually talking to multiple women at the same time. You'll know who they are because you'll see their status as "online" all day.

And last but not least is long-distance dating. I've heard about people who have met online and had long-distance relationships and ended up getting married. Long-distance dating is an option for you and can definitely work. It's just about putting in the time and effort to talk to each other regularly. I would do FaceTime, instead of direct messaging, because it's similar to being on a real date. You could even do a real date through FaceTime if you like. I suggest asking him a lot of questions to really get to know him and pay attention to his facial expressions and body language to gauge how honest or dishonest he's being. After a certain amount of time, if he suggests to meet up, make sure he's the one traveling to see you and not you traveling to see him. Your value will drop significantly if you put in this type of work just to see a man. You lower your value the more hoops you jump through, and this is a huge hoop! And just because he traveled far to see you doesn't mean he can sample your cookie! Don't let it crumble! I've participated in every type of dating I've discussed in this book, and I still prefer in person meetings.

CHAPTER 10
DATING DIVA

*"No matter how attractive a person's
potential may be you have to date their reality."*
~ Mandy Hale

Now that you're embodying your goddess within, the date requests are surely going to start pouring in. Before your date, you should be excited, not nervous. Nervous excitement is okay, but not too much. I remember dates I went on years ago, where I was all concerned about was whether the guy would like me. That's what women with low self-esteem do; they worry about being liked and desired and having their feelings hurt. When you're able to get past that, that's progress. Please don't even go on the date if you're worried about the guy liking you. Chances are, you won't totally be yourself if you are. Your concern should be about having fun and whether or not you like *him*. Hopefully you aren't dreading it. If it's a date you're dreading, don't go! Goddesses don't spend time with people they don't want to be around and never ever tolerate things they dislike. You should be looking forward to your date and thinking about having a good time.

Center yourself before you go out and make sure that you're going on this date for the right reason, which is to enjoy yourself. Remember, you're the prize, not him. He should be going out of his way to make you happy and not vice versa. Make it a point to remember that. If you're feeling nervous, do a quick meditation or breathing exercise and remind yourself that this is supposed to be fun! It's not supposed to feel like work or something you're dreading and if it is, review your reasons for going. Energy is contagious too. If you're feeling great, your energy will be felt by your date, whether consciously or not. Men always have a good time with a goddess!

When you start dating, don't look at each date as a potential Mr. Right. Instead, view your dates as an opportunity to have fun and practice what you've learned. We receive clarity through contrast. Clarity is a clear knowing of what we want, and contrast is knowing precisely what we don't want. By dating often, you will begin to get an idea of the kind of man you're looking for. The more you date, the more you can refine what you want in a man. When we know what it is that we don't want, it's that much easier to gain clarity for what we do want. I'm not suggesting you spend time with men you have no interest in. In fact, please don't do that. Goddesses utilize their time wisely and don't waste it. Time is a commodity and our most precious one at that! Be sure to screen each man before a date to ensure that he's someone worth spending your time with.

Don't go into any date thinking it'll be your last. Consider dating as a sport that you'd like to get good at. The more dates you go on, the more you will get a sense of what you want in a man and how to be a great date. I never see it as me needing to find someone, but rather, me seeing what's out there. I would never commit to a man unless he was someone that made me feel a way that no other man could. You're going to find that the stronger and more independent you become, the more you will need to raise your standards. When you become *more*, you desire to be with someone who is also *more*. Not just any old cutie will do, not anymore. It's important that you know what you're looking for in a man as well. Everything that we want exists and is ours for the taking. The only thing that can ever block our desires is our inability to believe in them. If you find yourself believing that what you want is hard to find, or not out there, it will be hard to find or non-existent, because you made it so. Again, like the famous saying goes, "Whether you say you can, or you cannot, you are correct." Our beliefs really do create our lives, so believe that what you want is possible! The simple fact of your believing in something makes its existence possible and inevitable. To not believe is only hurting and limiting you. Some women believe that all the good men are taken and that's simply not the case, but it will become their reality should they choose to continue believing that.

When I was younger, I thought it was attractive to dress provocatively. I thought that would make guys like me more, by wearing tight clothing and shirts that allowed for popping cleavage. Typically, its younger women who do this, simply due to a lack of experience and not knowing their value. It's for the attention. While you may think that this is what men want, it's not, not at all. Men prefer mystery and they know if you're showing it all, you're trying too hard. ***Women who have a lot to offer don't have to offer their bodies.*** Men like to think about unwrapping the gift and what the gift looks like behind the gift wrap. When you let all your goodies hang out, men don't get to use their imagination and spend time thinking about what you look like naked. You'd be surprised by how much time men spend thinking about what you look like naked! They say that if you've got it to flaunt it, but wouldn't you rather flaunt your brains than your body? Everyone has a body, but not everyone has brains. So, please use yours wisely. You can look gorgeous without having your boobs spilling out into your spaghetti! A classier guy will appreciate the time and effort you put into looking good. Dress to impress, like a college professor, that is! You can look beautiful without looking like a prostitute! Half-dressed girls are for weaker men who aren't willing to work for it. And if you've been doing the things outlined for you within these pages, you know that you're worth so much more than this. There are so many beautiful pieces of clothing in the world today. You don't need to show skin to look pretty. I remember being younger and hearing this very same thing, and I would think to myself, "You say that because you're older." Well, that may be true, but many times older does indeed mean wiser. Save the nudity for the bedroom and don't be in a hurry to get there too soon either. Dessert comes way after dinner!

Please don't go on one date and decide that "he is the one," and then stop dating all other men based on one single date. Go into each date with the sole purpose of having fun. The first guy you go out with may be great. But, compared to what? What if the second guy you went out with was going to be even better? And instead, you settled for guy number one because he seemed good enough? The thing is, you never know until you go. This is why I say to date a lot and to not get exclusive with anyone too soon. Please note, I did not suggest that you sleep around or sleep with any of your dates. I hope you don't. Unless that was all that you wanted from that guy. Again, I want you to think of dating as a sport. Even if you do well in the first quarter, you still have three more quarters to go! Just imagine if the man of your dreams doesn't show up until the eighth date, and you've already committed to the guy from date number three? What do you do? I can't make that choice for you. All I can suggest is that you keep your options open.

If any of your dates ask you if you're seeing anyone else, please be honest. Tell them that you're in no hurry to be exclusive with anyone and that, yes, you are seeing other people. Even if you haven't met anyone else just yet, you will. Most people respect honesty, even if it isn't exactly what they wanted to hear. Just remember, if he dates other women, you can't get upset. You shouldn't be attached to any of these guys so soon either. It takes a long time to get to know a person and many people, unfortunately, aren't themselves upon an initial meeting. Take your time with this and don't be in a hurry to settle down. Guys can sense when you're in a hurry and not present in the moment just enjoying your time together. And if you're holding out for marriage, keep dating until you become exclusive with someone who you know also wants to get married. Don't stop going on dates until you've met someone you're positive about spending your time or life with.

People are overly concerned with what other people think about them on a crazy level. Keep an open mind when meeting new people and remember, dating is supposed to be fun! If you're all stressed out, ask yourself your reasons for wanting to go on this date. Is it so you can lock him in before your 30th birthday, get that ring, and pop those babies out? If so, please re-examine your values. Living a life of value begins with valuing yourself. Never do something because everyone else is doing it. Crowd followers only go as far as the crowd goes. Ask yourself your reasons for wanting what you want. Each reason should be intrinsic and come from inside you, which means you should have feelings attached to those desires. Never do anything because everyone else is doing it or because someone else told you that you should. The only person who can truly guide you on the right path for you is you. Always listen to your instincts about a person too. If something feels "off" about a guy, chances are that sooner or later, you will find out why. That's a red flag and needs to be addressed. Always speak up and ask questions if you get an "off feeling" from him. Asking him to elaborate will help you learn more. Don't be afraid to throw that fish back if he's hiding things or through conversation you learn things about him that are on your list of dealbreakers! I never ignore my feelings because they have never steered me wrong. Bottom line is don't be so quick to be exclusive. Take your time and enjoy yourself along the way.

Only become exclusive when it feels right and you have really gotten some dating experience under your belt, to see who is out there. Obviously, the man you choose to be exclusive with should be someone you're also in love with. Crazy chemistry in the beginning is a red flag because typically that means that you've both endured a similar type of childhood trauma, which makes you drawn to each other like a moth to a flame! This type of chemistry burns out quickly but is a TON of fun in the beginning. Please don't fall for it. The crazier the chemistry is, the more likely you share a traumatic childhood experience. Make sure you're doing the inner work we've discussed so you can see this coming from a mile away. Never be afraid to speak up and ask the important questions that need to be asked. Chemistry and compatibility are two very different things. Chemistry is like an electrical magnetism while compatibility is more about how well you two will get along together in a relationship.

I've mentioned a few times now that a date should be fun. Fun usually includes laughter, and hopefully some interesting conversation. It can also include entertainment, activities, food, music, nature, and any other number of things. Fun is fun, simply put. While a date is supposed to be an opportunity to get to know a person, it's not meant to be a counseling session. Leave your baggage behind. In fact, if you're feeling very emotional, do yourself a favor and reschedule. How would you feel going on a date with a guy who complained to you about his awful life the entire time? If you just said to yourself, "I don't know, I've been through worse, it doesn't sound all that bad," then you're still being a doormat who doesn't think she deserves happiness. You're not ready to date. People go out to have a good time, not to be a shoulder to cry on. There are professionals out there who get paid to listen to people's problems. Your date, even if he is a shrink, is going out with you to enjoy your company. Crying in your wine isn't fun for anyone. I'm not one for formalities, so, I prefer when things develop naturally. Super formal dates where the guy hurls 20 questions at you about your life and who you are and where you see yourself in five or 10 years feel like work or a job interview – NO THANKS! I'd have more fun at home watching a movie with my cat! Not to say that these types of dates can't go well. I'm sure they can. I just personally don't enjoy these types of dates at all. And I've also learned that if a guy has this type of routine up front, chances always end up that he just is not for me. As you get better, you can catch the signs earlier. The more the guy likes you, the more thought and effort he will put into your dates. If a guy takes you to a strip club or boxing match for your first date, please make sure it's your last date with him! He should be trying to impress you, so you want to see him again. He should also be interested in learning who you are and asking you questions about what you like and what your preferences are so he can strive to impress you, so he can get that second date!

So, how do you stop yourself from becoming a "Date Dud?" You stay in the moment. Be present and never be in your head! Look around you and notice what you see. Check out the atmosphere. Is there music playing where you are? Are you out for dinner? How is the food? Comment on the entertainment or how good the food is or discuss some amazing thing that you have always wanted to do or try! The key is to have fun, feel good, and be excited about what comes next! Getting the facts on the table is boring. SNORE. While it may be important to know that your date does have an income and a place to live, you don't need to discuss these things all night long. We like being around people who make us feel good and answering a long list of questions just never feels very good to me. A date should never feel *hard*. If it does, you're doing it wrong. I don't know anyone who loves a deep conversation more than myself. This kind of pressure on a first date is unnecessary though. Once you get to know a person, ask away! But, for starters, keep it light and keep it fun. Don't talk about your problems and don't complain about your life either. People like to be around happy people.

Being yourself is the best way to go. I'm always myself, no matter what. If people don't like me, that's their problem. If you aren't yourself, you're going to waste precious time. How would you like it if your date wasn't himself? If he put on a false front, of being someone that he thought you would like, only to find out who he really is years later? So many people pretend too and then end up divorced several years later when they finally decide to be themselves and their spouse doesn't end up liking their true self! Don't do that to another person. You shouldn't be so desperate for love. If you are, you're not ready for the right kind of love that will feed your soul. Rejection is only a form of redirection. I promise you that there is someone out there for you. Don't sell yourself short by latching onto the first guy you feel a spark with. Fires don't last forever, but unconditional love does!

Please don't start dating until you're ready. Only you will know when that time is. If you're acting desperate or secretly hoping the first guy you go out with will fall madly in love with you, you're not ready yet. I'm sorry to be the one to say it, but I don't want you to waste time being exclusive with Mr. Wrong. Using clarity through contrast, we determine what it is that we don't want, to discover what it is that we do want and shift our focus from feelings of lack to feelings of having in the now. Once we know what not to do on a date, it's time to consider then the right things to do. Being yourself is just assumed, always. Remember that because it's important. What qualities make you attractive to men? I'd say that it depends on the man himself. But, as a rule, people want to feel excited and alive. So many people are living complacent lives, doing the same boring things day in and day out, just to keep a roof over their heads and food on the table. Going out should be an escape from all of that and a chance to let off some steam. The real you is precisely what everyone is after. However, the real you may be hidden behind layers of fears, insecurities, false beliefs, society's expectations, programming, trying to fit in, and other unconscious things. If I could give you one tip to make your date better, it'd be to free yourself. Step out of your responsibilities, moral obligations, and professional appearances. The three qualities that will allow you to be yourself, have a good time, and get a call for a second date are as follows:

- Be Mysterious
- Be Fun
- Be Unpredictable

Are you being mysterious when you talk about your problems with your date? No. Mystery is "not knowing" something. Never put all your cards on the table up front. Being real and being honest are not the same as *telling all*. Your private life is private, and just for you. In no way are you obligated to share every little detail. Learn to be tight-lipped with certain things and free and open with others. Have you ever been around a person who can talk endlessly? When you talk endlessly like this, it's an emotional response. People with childhood traumas or other types of problems in life feel the need to talk a lot. When you talk endlessly like this, you leave nothing to wonder about. You've shared everything you possibly could, and then some. So, what's left for him to think about? If you give it all away, you take away his opportunity to figure you out, and that's where most of the fun is for men. Usually, people who are that talkative are lonely and looking for a connection and will try anyone with an open ear. The cute guy you just met at the coffee shop is not the right person to vent to. You do that with a close friend, family member, or a therapist. Men like to think about you when they aren't with you and wonder about you. If you've already told him all that there is to know about you, what have you left for him to wonder about? Always leave them wanting more and wondering more. Did you get that? Leave them wondering and wanting. Doing that requires that you stay tight lipped about certain things and cut the date short. You're not obligated to answer every question he asks either. Feel free to be a sly minx who changes the topic. No matter how great of a time you're having, **go home early**. Always leave him wanting more. Besides, you need your own down time after dinner. You can say you have an early day if he asks, but again, goddesses don't explain themselves to anyone. The less he knows about you, the more you will be on his mind!

At the same time, don't sit there being all quiet and shy. No one wants that either. Those are two extremes that you should avoid at all costs. Surely, you're not a mouse and you are capable of speech. Confidence comes with time and once you have that, you have everything. A strong woman will talk when she wants to talk and be silent when she wants to be silent. Be comfortable with long silent pauses and never feel the need to close the gap by talking. That's his job. Never feel that you're responsible for carrying the conversation. Silent pauses can be quite comforting because they show a certain level of comfort and that's attractive. Trying too hard is another sign of low self-esteem. You overdo it because your self-worth is not what it should be and so you try to overcompensate. A quality man will notice that fairly quickly and quite possibly lose interest in you. Get comfortable with silent moments. You don't need to fill them. Any woman who tries too hard does so because she feels like she is less, and therefore, must do *more* to impress a man or sustain a relationship. Nothing could be further from the truth.

You never, I repeat, never, ever, go out of your way for a man! Doing so will only show him how little value you have placed on yourself. If you go into an exclusive relationship with a man like this, know that you will be the one who is more interested and putting more effort into the relationship. You won't be happy, and you will likely be taking on the masculine role of "doing" in the relationship. Sound familiar? I've only learned all the right things to do because I've already done all the wrong things. It's clarity through contrast. After a while, it all comes quite naturally.

Before you can walk, you must crawl. I started gaining confidence by flirting. I never really knew how to do it. I had a friend who I'd had a crush on, and he flirted with me something fierce. I liked him and I wasn't afraid, so I flirted right back. You just need a bit of confidence and playfulness. The really wonderful thing about flirting is that it can be taken at least two different ways. Some men will think you have a genuine interest in them. But the smarter ones will know that this may very well just be your personality. Now, I am not suggesting you flirt with strangers when you're in an exclusive relationship but do feel free to flirt with everyone while you're single. I love flirting. It's fun, free, and it's harmless. It keeps them guessing too. I remember playing the "he said this," or "he did that," game and asking friends, "What does it mean?" When you reach a certain level of confidence, you don't do that anymore because you don't invest that much of your time into wondering if a man likes you. If a man truly likes you, you will know! If he hasn't made it known to you yet or denies having feelings for you, MOVE ON. I can't stress that enough. Please never waste your time on any one man. I don't care if you've known him for 20 years or if you are best friends or even if he is your everything. If you were his everything, the two of you would already be together! Don't fool yourself.

Lately, there's a lot of information available about attracting or manifesting your "SP" or your specific person. If a man doesn't have a genuine interest and investment in you, he will never treat you the way you deserve to be treated. So why try to manifest a specific man? If he liked you at all, you'd be together now. Never try to manifest a specific person. A specific person is another term for a "specific pattern." We tend to seek out relationships that feel familiar to those from childhood, despite the toxicity. He doesn't see you as a high value woman and that's okay, because there's plenty of men out there who will. Remember what I said before; rejection is just another form of redirection. You never chase a man under any circumstances. Women who value themselves never do this. Doing this lowers your worth and your value and makes you feel like complete crap on top of everything else! An SP will never treat you like the goddess that you are because you've already shown him your true colors and they're not goddess colors. Be sure you've done your own inner healing to avoid attracting a partner who is unhealed from childhood or past traumas because we're always attracting who we are on the inside. The law of attraction is about being a mirror or living in a mirrored universe where each person we meet will reflect certain aspects of ourselves.

I don't care what the circumstances are, but if after a certain amount of time passes and he hasn't been direct and up front with you about his feelings or his intentions, BUH-BYE. Don't let the door hit you on the ass on your way out! You are a Goddess and Goddesses don't wait for Mr. Maybe to grace them with a word. We move on and we move up. If you find yourself stewing over a guy for an extended period, let him go. If a guy genuinely is interested in you, you don't need to wait years to learn that. And if you sit around waiting on any man, that's your own fault! If he likes you and wants to be with you, he will find a way to let you know. If he doesn't find a way to express his feelings for you, he's too weak-minded for you or not the right guy. Either way, move on. Don't waste years of your life on a maybe because you can't see the better guy waiting in your future. I PROMISE YOU, he is there, if you just believe. Practice flirting with guy friends if that's more comfortable for you. If you're open enough, you can really have fun with it. Maybe some of you don't know what flirting is. For those who are inexperienced, I will throw one out there for you. Let's say that your friends with a guy you like, and you two text each other daily. Chances are you joke with one another. Throwing words on the end of sentences or phrases like, "jerk," believe it or not, are forms of flirting. It may be a little sarcastic flirting, but still flirting. Surely, someone has flirted with you at least once in your life. You know how it feels. You've probably been on the receiving end of a guy's flirting and asked yourself what it means. Sure, sometimes it means he is interested in you. But, like myself, and so many others, it might just be his personality. Get to know a person to determine if they're flirting or "just talking," because it can go either way. Learn how to flirt with men and be sure to have fun with it. You can always practice on dating apps!

Another quality that makes people feel good is spending time with someone who is easy-going and down-to Earth. In other words, let your guard down and be someone that others feel they can talk to. Bring those walls down because it's time to play! Guys like women who are playful and take risks. Of course, there are times in life when we need to be serious, but dating just isn't one of them. Leave your serious face at home and drop those walls. You should be smiling and laughing frequently to show you're having a good time. You won't get very far if you don't. Men can sense when a woman is emotionally unavailable and vice versa. Be as vulnerable as possible, without revealing too much about yourself. Roll with the punches and be in the moment. Think about a woman you know that effortlessly attracts men. I'd bet that she is incredibly secure with who she is, she seems relaxed and she's almost always smiling. It's not because she was born with a silver spoon in her mouth, but likely because she learned the hard way. This book isn't just a recipe for attracting love, but also, a better life. Being playful is good and takes a lot of the pressure off on a date. Consider past dates that you've been on, and which ones felt good, and which ones felt not so good. I bet the best dates were the ones where you were being yourself, being open, and flexible. I guess the best way to say it is just "lighten up." Don't take things seriously or personally. It shouldn't feel like work, not at all.

Confident women know how to tease men. Men love to be teased. To say yes, then very quickly to change your mind and say no. This type of behavior keeps men on the edge of their seats and can drive them crazy in a fantastic way! When your concern is more on how *you* feel, than on how he feels, your confidence will soar. In the movie filmed mainly in France, titled, *French Kiss* with Meg Ryan and Kevin Kline, he teaches her how to win her fiancé back. At one point, the two of them are eavesdropping on a couple's conversation at an outdoor café. One moment, the woman is happy and smiling, and the next, she looks miserable, pouty, and looks away from the man. Meg Ryan doesn't like this, and she says, "I don't get that. What is it with French women? They say no when they mean yes. If you're happy you smile, if you're sad you frown." Kevin Kline then goes on to explain to her how men love being kept in this constant suspension state of excitement and confusion. Seductresses know that's the recipe for drawing a man in. If you've got a man both excited and confused at the same time, and he was already interested in you, he's yours for the taking! It's got to be real though. Fakeness and games will only sustain you for so long. When your priority is *not* to please a man, you can focus more on pleasing yourself. A strong woman knows she can always change her mind and will do so if the situation requires it. Men actually love when we are ourselves and being real. Being a doormat or a pushover is so old school and will only help you to stay single. You'd be much better off by being a "difficult" woman. Go out there and have fun, be flirty, be playful, and be mysterious. Be fabulous!

Communication is probably the biggest make or break factor in a relationship. Effective communication is crucial to sustain any good relationship. Too much or too little will kill it before it begins. And while you should leave it to the man to make and plan dates with you, the way you respond and interact with him in between dates is incredibly important! The way you communicate on the first few dates versus how you will communicate in an exclusive relationship may differ, but there are certain things you'll want to avoid saying or doing. In this amazing article from the web site altaredmarriage.com, they discuss five communication killers and how to avoid them. I will briefly discuss them with you here because as we both know women tend to downplay times they're displeased and not speak up. In the big scheme of things, you can choose to bite your tongue and sit back and suck it up or stand up and speak up! The first no-no in dating communication is called "minimizing," where your date or partner will express something they're unhappy with or that's causing them pain. Responding with something like, "Oh that's not that bad," or "I've had worse," is a way of minimizing the way the other person feels, and you never want to do this! All feelings are valid, yours and his. The second communication killer is a big one that a lot of people do and it's "defensiveness," and comes in many forms. A few examples of this are: anger, attacking, pouting, silent treatment, excuses, justifications, and explanations. I've already discussed how we should never be explaining ourselves, so this reinforces that. Giving another person the silent treatment is literally a form of emotional abuse! This article states that:

"Defensiveness communicates to the other person that you are closed off to their feedback or input and aren't willing to hear anything about your behavior. Defensiveness does not necessarily stem from the belief that the person is not wrong, but often shows up because the person already feels badly about themselves or their behavior, and receiving more confirmation of their inability to measure up can be overwhelming. Rather than feeling worse about this area of themselves, they would rather defend and deflect so they don't have to continue feeling bad."

The third communication killer in dating and relationships is sarcasm. The article states that,

"As fun and light-hearted as sarcasm may seem, to others it often communicates disdain and disrespect. The things another person may communicate and feel passionate about should not become the foundation of another's jokes. Sarcasm hurts people, closes people's hearts and takes healthy conversations in a painful direction many times. The use of sarcasm can often be a passive-aggressive way to confront others."

The fourth communication crusher is using universal statements such as "always" or "never." It's stated that:

"There are certainly situations where your partner accidentally got it right or didn't get it wrong, so when you use statements like 'always' or 'never' it simply isn't true. The other person will then ignore or discount everything else you're going to communicate because they don't agree that 'they always' or 'they never' do that thing that you're bringing up. The other problem with universal statements is they cause the person to feel hopeless. You are likely bringing up the issue because you desire change in this area. When you use the words 'always' and 'never,' it communicates total failure. The other person is thinking to themselves, 'If I never get it right or always get it wrong then what's the point of even trying?' Rather than being receptive to your feedback and trying to improve in this area they will just give up."

People don't like to hear that they're rigid, even if it's true, so try not to use the universal statements on your dates or in your relationships ever. Communication killer number five is what is termed "Shutdown Statements," where you say something that basically kills the conversation, and most times just isn't true. These statements show up when we're feeling hurt, angry, or overwhelmed and as the article states, "They are the verbal equivalent of shutting the door in someone's face." Here are five shutdown statements:

1. "It's fine" (when it's not fine with you)
2. "Nothing" (when it's something)
3. "I can't do anything right"
4. "It doesn't matter" (when it does matter to you)
5. "You're right" (when you don't believe they are right)

Some other forms of communication you may want to avoid using include the following: raising your voice, interrupting, being passive aggressive, holding grudges, guessing the other person's feelings, any type of name calling, making threats, avoiding problems rather than discussing them, and repeatedly arguing about the same thing. Most of these things won't typically occur in the early stages of dating, but you want to be aware that you're never doing these things as they can cause unfixable damage to your relationship!

And ladies, while we're on the topic, if a man asks you what's wrong, DO NOT tell him, "Nothing," because he will believe you! Sorry to be the one to break it to you, but they're not mind readers. You hope that your guy will have that sixth sense or keen intuition and just know that you have a problem and what it is, but they don't. If you have a problem, say so! Otherwise, you will continue to have that problem. Open and honest communication is the key to making a relationship work. Being honest and staying real go together. Speaking up about how you feel and having a voice is crucial. If you go along with and agree with everything he says and all his choices, you're being a boring doormat again and he will quickly lose interest! You'll also be incredibly unhappy, if even at an unconscious level. Men require you to have an "edge" and a mental toughness. You know who you are and what you want and you're not afraid to let them know!

Good ways to communicate involve being clear by using "I" statements to express your needs and wants, such as "I need" or "I feel." Your partner will easily understand you and know what you want when you speak this way. Be sure to be empathetic by trying to understand your partner's feelings, needs, and intentions. Listen to them without judgment. Make sure you're vulnerable enough to be open and share your thoughts and feelings with them. Being vulnerable is crucial so make sure that you're being vulnerable when it's necessary. Many people never allow themselves to be vulnerable due to being hurt in the past so many times! Don't share too much in the beginning, but once you're in a relationship, this is a necessity. When necessary, ask open-ended questions to learn more about them. Always be present and try to pick up on non-verbal clues and body language. Usually when someone crosses their arms it can mean that they're not open so look out for that and try to ease their feelings.

Be sure to accept responsibility for your own feelings and not blame him for how you feel, even if you feel tempted to do so. Most of these communication tips won't come up on a first date but know that it's always good to ask questions and be present. Keep these tips in mind for when you do get into a good relationship. No one is perfect and sometimes we misunderstand things. It's good to know these communication tips in advance. Before you're ever tempted to overreact, please consider coming back to this list of communication tips and to be present and thoughtful in how you communicate, especially if you're feeling upset.

CHAPTER 11
HOLD ONTO YOUR COOKIE!

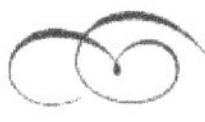

"I will not be triumphed over."
~ Cleopatra

I have an interesting story to start this chapter. One day, I was at my grandmother's house with my boyfriend, and we were looking at a picture of my grandma from when she was younger with my mom as a child. My boyfriend was standing behind my grandma, and he was making sexual gestures behind her back! Mind you, my grandma was 91 years old. When we left, he said to me, "Your grandma was hot back in her day, I would've given it to her good!" I laughed as that was just hysterical. Later, I told my grandma that story and what he said, and she got a good laugh, too. Then she said, "I was quite the cookie back in my day!" Now, I'm guessing she meant it to mean that she was quite the tasty morsel, or very attractive looking. I liked the terminology she used and have decided to use it here in my own way.

Although, when I use the word "cookie," we both know what I'm referring to. For the lack of a better word, it's your power center. Keep it, and you keep your power contained within you. Give it away and you become vulnerable and attached. Not only that but give it up too soon and you risk never seeing the guy again, as most guys won't stay interested in a woman with no mystery who gives it up that easily. Now, there are some women in existence who can have sex and remain emotionally detached, but it's just not the norm. It's also not safe or advisable. As women, our emotions tend to get the best of us. Additionally, men don't typically respect women who sleep with them on the first few dates. When you sleep with a guy on a first date, he assumes you do this with all men and you're immediately viewed as a low value woman. And so many of us women have spent so much time trying to find "the one," that we can get attached to a man rather quickly. And while sex might feel great, it doesn't feel great to never hear from the guy again, does it? I know sometimes if you feel the guy isn't a high value man you might say screw it and sleep with him just to get yours because you have no interest in seeing him again. Please reconsider your own value before sharing your body with a man you barely know. Whenever we exchange bodily fluids with another human being, it takes seven years for that energy to leave you!

How about being disrespected? That doesn't feel very good either. All that strength you worked so hard to create inside of you—gone for a fleeting moment of physical pleasure. A natural seductress can pull this off because she knows how to stay detached. Cleopatra was a natural seductress, and often slept with men immediately, as it was one of her ways to draw them in. She had control of herself though and she was far smarter than the men she slept with. Cleopatra had emotional control (and a plan), which is a huge difference. Men respect women who respect themselves. It's that simple. I've literally had men say to me, "Do you know why I respect you so much? It's because I can see how much you respect yourself."

To make your life simpler, just assume that all men are interested in you, whether it's true or not. It simplifies things. It leaves out the wondering and allows you to go directly to the action step. Assume they all want you and you can treat them as they should be treated. If one doesn't like you, move onto the next. But at least this way, you will be prepared if someone asks you out. You don't owe anyone anything either. Never feel obligated to share your cookie with anyone or your time. When I began to assume that every man I met or knew, either wanted a date or sex, I was always prepared. Assume every man you meet wants in—your pants that is! You must be smart and be prepared. This isn't about ego or thinking you're wonderful or better than anyone else. It's about understanding men and understanding ourselves and using that to our advantage. You always need to keep yourself safe and never think that other people think the same way you do or that someone isn't willing to hurt you. Men value women who present them with a challenge and don't ever value women who don't. Your value is in the chase. The harder the man has to work to pursue you or sleep with you, the more valuable you will become to him.

Don't be in such a hurry to jump into bed with a guy you barely know. Even if you know him well, how well do you know his intentions? Men will act differently if they think it'll get you to sleep with them. Also, they will say or do just about anything to get you to have sex with them! Never assume that another person thinks or feels the way you do. The only way to keep your cookie from crumbling is to hold onto it and hold out. You may be asking yourself now, "Is that all men want, my cookie?" Well, some yes, unfortunately. It does work both ways though. Anyone who gets chased will naturally run away. It's just human nature. The lesson in this is that men will spend a considerable amount of time with you, trying to get you into bed with them. Now, this isn't to say that they don't genuinely like you. Of course, there will be some men who genuinely like you and do want more than just sex from you. Only time will tell though. The only way to determine which guys only want sex from you and which guys are looking for an actual relationship is by waiting and not putting out. I think it was Ali Wong, in one of her stand-up specials, who said she didn't even kiss her husband until their fifth date! Now, that's one smart goddess right there!

In the end, only you will know what is best for you. Don't go asking your girlfriends if they think it's okay for the two of you to sleep together yet. Her opinion really doesn't matter. It's a decision only you can make when the time is right. Please just don't rush into it. You don't want to be seen as low-value or desperate. It should only happen when it feels like it must, not because you both had too much to drink, or it was a great second date. Only you have been there with him through it all and only you know how you feel and what you want. Please remember how easily we women can get attached to a guy, especially if we're having a lot of fun with him. Don't think that men are like you. While some may be, many are just trying to get laid. Men don't fantasize about getting married or having kids. Mostly their fantasies involving you probably contain nudity and no cakes or baby rattles. There are those hopeless romantic men who are in love with love. But do you really want to be with someone who would be happy to be with any warm bodied female? I wouldn't. You shouldn't want a man in your life to ever fill a void. It should always be to add to your life and make it better. The number of dates or number of anything shouldn't have any influence on when or even if you decide to sleep with a man.

The best way to make sure you keep your cookie from crumbling is to go home alone. This sounds so much easier than it really is though. Depending on the guy, they can be quite manipulative. "Can I come in for five minutes, I'd like to use your restroom?" If it's not the bathroom, then they might ask to come in for a drink. Don't give them an inch. Say, "I have to be up early and need to go now." The thing is you don't owe him anything. No excuse is necessary. A strong woman can say no and mean it, without feeling the need to give an explanation or feel bad about it. If you think you've got to let him sample your cookie because he bought you some chicken, think again. Many guys these days don't even take women on real dates! Don't bother with this type of man because he has nothing to offer you. It's all in what you choose to accept. However, there are men who do want a relationship and love, so, don't give up hope. I wouldn't even let him in to use the bathroom. Depending on how well you know the guy, do you really want to take the risk? I mean, if you just met this guy a few days ago and this was a first date, what's stopping him from raping you and killing you once he's inside your house? Be smart. Don't just protect your cookie from crumbling, but also, protect your life from ending. Always use your intuition around new people. Ask yourself what feels right or what feels safe? If you get the slightest inkling that something is "off," be on high alert. Always drive yourself to meet your dates so if things aren't going well, you'll always have the opportunity to leave. If you don't have a car, make sure you can get an Uber or Lyft to get a ride home.

If your date acts offensively, you can always excuse yourself and leave. Women with high values and standards wouldn't sit through an entire meal with someone they knew was a waste of their time!

One thing that I am noticing more these days is men trying to get women to come to "house dates." This is where a guy asks you out, but only to his house. If you're lucky, he might make you some mac n' cheese or something before he starts trying to touch you. Don't say I didn't warn you. Smart women never agree to a house date! You'd be trapping yourself in an unsafe environment with an unknown person. Furthermore, no self-respecting female says yes to a house date unless you're already a couple or close to it. If a new guy tries getting you to come to his house for dinner **JUST SAY NO**. Sometimes, they end up not even cooking any food and acting all nonchalant about it. It ends up being a rouse just to get you naked. If you do say yes, you know what it tells the guy about you? It tells him that you're low-maintenance and probably easy too. Are you easy? No, you say? Then, don't act like it. Never say yes to a house date. You should never be working to impress a man or wondering if he likes you. Your thoughts should always be on how you feel and what you want. House dates are for real relationships, not for first dates. Hold out for someone who goes out of their way to make you feel special and plans special dates just for you.

Again, I feel I need to mention something about safety here. If you're dating a lot, make sure you have a close friend or family member who you talk to daily, who you can tell where you're going. Someone needs to know your location. Better safe than sorry. Make sure each time you go out with someone new, that someone knows where you will be going and who you will be with. We live in a very crazy and unpredictable world these days. Make sure your dates are meeting you at public places and not planning midnight picnics in the forest. Don't assume that the man you're with is a good person. Hopefully, he is wonderful. But would you bet your life on it? Play it safe by always being in public places and not putting yourself in sketchy circumstances. If something feels wrong, it probably is. It's not worth the risk. If a guy likes you, he won't stop liking you because you said no. If anything, he will like you even more. Never be afraid to say no. Men love a challenge! Again, you owe him absolutely nothing! If a man is truly interested in you, the word no will just propel him try harder to win you over. Like I mentioned before, men love a challenge and any who deny that they do, are lying. If a guy truly likes you, nothing on this planet will stop him from spending time with you, so, please never feel obligated. You need to be your own priority, every single time.

I've already discussed getting men to jump through hoops for you repeatedly, but it does need to be discussed again, pertaining to this section. You can't give your cookie away or give out free samples if you're truly interested in someone. You will have given him his trophy, after he didn't even participate in the competition! Not only did he not win, but he didn't even play, and you still rewarded him? How much do you think he is going to go out of his way for you in the future now? No one appreciates *something for nothing*, not really. And if you don't think you are a prize, think again! He wouldn't be taking you out if he didn't see you as a prize. You have to make him earn it! He has to work for it and prove his worthiness. I don't care how old-fashioned or outdated this might sound. Some things stay true forever. This is one of those things. No one appreciates something for nothing, nobody. How satisfied do you feel after working super hard at something and reaching your goal? It feels phenomenal, right? Imagine getting something you wanted desperately, but doing nothing to get it? How much would you appreciate it in the future? We only appreciate the things we work for and put effort in towards. Women need to find themselves again and stop giving it away. That begins with valuing yourself and safeguarding your cookie! When starting something new with someone, remember it's your power center. Consider how soon in the relationship you'd like to give your power away. There are times to be vulnerable and this isn't one of them.

How do you preserve your cookie? Learn this word well: NO. Use it frequently. When you tell someone no, it should be firm. There are some persistent men who feel entitled to an answer or explanation. Explaining yourself to anyone, for any reason, is a power stealer. A simple **no** should always suffice. My point is that you don't owe anyone an answer. If a guy asks to come into your place and you don't want him to, the conversation should end after you say no. If the guy gets pushy, realize this will be your last date with this guy. No one has the right to make you do anything you don't want to do ever. A strong woman can say no and leave it at that. Consider bringing some pepper spray just to be safe.

You need to have really high standards. I don't care what your standards were in the past. That was then, this is now. Now you're a high-maintenance Goddess who is desired by men everywhere. Men, when given the chance, would love to shower you with romance and gifts. You no longer settle, and you don't try to mold any man into being "the one." In this lifetime, we have multiple "soul mates," not just one. Never feel like you lost your one and only chance. You have many chances and many mates. A real soul mate is a person you have spent time with in past lifetimes and it could be in any capacity. So, don't get caught up on your "one and only," because there's tons of those available for you. Be strong in your convictions and don't feel obligated to supply answers.

I do need you to raise your standards. If need be, go back to the chapter on spending time alone. If you can't be comfortable being with yourself, you will tolerate a lot of things and people that you don't want to. If you have a fulfilling life, nothing is missing. When you can occupy, utilize, and enjoy all your time, you really don't need anyone else. I'm not advocating a martyr lifestyle. I just don't want you to lower your standards just to have someone else around. We've all done it. We've all been there and dated someone we weren't very interested in just because we thought it was better than being alone. Why is it better than being alone? I absolutely love spending time alone. In fact, I don't know a single person who I have a better time with than I do with myself. It may sound selfish, but I made my life that way. And when you can make your life that way, you no longer settle. You don't have to count on other people for any single part of your happiness. When that happens, it's a game changer! Do you want to be accountable for your own happiness or would you rather it lay in the hands of someone else? When you expect someone else to make you happy, they can feel that, and they always end up resenting you for it because it's not their job to make you happy. It's your job to make you happy.

If a guy isn't everything you dreamed of, and then some, throw that fish back! I'm serious about the "and then some" part too. That means that not only is he everything you've wanted, but he is also better than the best you could have imagined for yourself. Imagination is huge in creating your life. Remember to believe in what you imagine too, or you won't see it. Once you decide to stop settling, the real magic can begin. Have you ever heard the saying, "If you can believe it, you can achieve it?" It's quite true. Do you believe that you deserve someone amazing? You need to **feel it**. Do you feel that you deserve someone amazing? Do you feel that you're someone amazing? Please don't start dating until you can answer that question with a *yes*. Furthermore, I'd rather spend the rest of my life alone than with someone who isn't better than the best I can imagine. You should be more than okay with being alone or you may find yourself settling. The only guarantee that you have against settling is loving yourself enough. Date anyone you like, but never enter into an exclusive relationship with someone who is less than everything you've ever wanted. See every man you encounter as a potential friend, someone to get to know, have fun with, and nothing more. And I don't mean, "just for now," while secretly pining away for them hoping it all comes together down the road. Chances are that many of them will be attracted to you or want to date you. But what they want doesn't matter, now does it? All that matters is what you want! Really let that sink in. Some of these men can turn into dates or even lifetime friends.

Sex is not love. It might feel great and solidify a bond between two people, but it's not love. Not even close. It's an expression of love when you're actually in love with each other. Granted, we are sexual creatures by nature and enjoy it for what it is. Just please use your discretion and best judgement when it comes to choosing who you sleep with. It might feel right in the moment but leave you feeling terrible afterwards. I'm no prude, so, I'm not going to tell you to never do it. I just don't want you to give yourself away too early or to the wrong person. It's always going to come down to a judgement call that only you can make. Use your gut, your intuition, to help you decide. Just know that having sex does not get you love. If anything, it's the opposite. Please remember that. People always put on their best face for first dates, so make sure you date worthwhile men for a while before deciding to sleep with one. Definitely don't sleep with more than one man at a time either.

On a last note, I need to tell you something important. Men will say ANYTHING to get you to have sex with them. ANYTHING. If your specific pattern with men is showing up in your life again or you find yourself entertaining a man you know is all wrong for you, please, for the love of God, don't have sex with that man! Men and women are not the same when it comes to sex. Women get emotionally attached after they become physically intimate with a man and men don't. Please don't tell yourself that you're the exception and you can tell you have a "special bond" with him. Or that you can tell he is changing for you in ways to make your life easier. Don't make justifications for his lousy behavior. Watch to see that his actions and behaviors line up. Your higher self is testing you and you're failing if you keep letting this man invest in you.

If a man tells you he's not the marrying kind, believe him! And if you are looking for marriage, say so! It doesn't mean you're telling him you want to marry him, but it lets him know what you want in your life in the future and hopefully stops him from wasting your time if he wants something different. When people tell you who they are, believe them the first time. It'll save you tons of stress and heartbreak. I've watched too many women repeat their pattern and justify to me why to even count. It's all emotional. And there's a payoff they're getting or they wouldn't be doing it. If your friends and family are all telling you the guy's awful, chances are he likely is. Regarding sex, when in doubt, always go without!

CHAPTER 12
EMOTIONAL INTELLIGENCE

Your emotions and the degree of control you have over them will directly affect your life in a huge way, especially in your relationships with others. Your emotions can only control you if you let them. You are not your emotions. Emotions are meant to guide. Emotions should be felt, processed, and released. Emotions are a form of information. You acknowledge and feel them and move on. As I'm sure you know, we tend to get stuck in some of the painful emotions for longer than we'd like. The amount of emotional intelligence that you possess will impact your life in every possible way. And in relationships, emotions can make or break them. Logic is great, but your heart's desires don't live in your brain, so you will need to develop some emotional intelligence and discipline. Decide right now that you will control yourself emotionally. When I say, "control yourself," I mean to not let your emotions run wild or get out of hand. You control your emotions. You do not allow them to control you. How do you do this? Practice. Lots and lots of practice. We're all works in progress, and we all have feelings. Allowing your feelings to control you is like living life on autopilot or by default. It's being unconscious and unaware. I promise that you are stronger than whatever it is that you're feeling, you just need to believe it. Once you realize that you're stronger than anything that life throws at you, emotional control will be a lot easier.

Even if you're sensitive like myself, you can still control the surplus of energy that you feel inside of you, even if it seems overwhelming at times. If you can manage to cultivate a feeling of inner peace at your core, things won't bother you as much, because during troubling times you can focus on and center on this inner peace inside of you. I've found that meditation helps tremendously with this. The purpose of meditation is to bring you into the now. We should all be in the now, but most of us are living inside of our thoughts. Thinking seems to take us out of time, don't you think? Meditation is new to me so when I can fully concentrate and stop thinking, it feels amazing! The only moment we ever truly have is always right now.

Learn to be so calm and unshakable internally that nothing that happens outside of you can rattle you or get you to react emotionally. **Always pause before answering a question or responding as this removes any emotional charge that you may have regarding a situation.** The more present you are, the less thoughts you need to think and the more embodied you become. With embodiment comes peace and obviously, presence. Thinking causes you to leave your body for the moment. You're not fully present when you're in your head. Just think of the last time you were in a conversation with someone, and your mind started to wander because something they said reminded you of something else and the person might have had to stop and say, "Are you still listening?" You checked out of that conversation by thinking about something else. Presence and embodiment are incredibly important. Be present by being mindful. Live in the present moment always.

When you live inside your head, you don't experience the now. Right now is always your point of power. Thinking takes you out of the moment. Future life events will occur based on precisely how you are feeling in the now. Being in your head most of the time doesn't make you such great company either. People who are always in their heads very seldom pay attention to what is going on around them. They've removed themselves from time! You know exactly what I'm referring to. Just think about the people in your life. I bet you know someone who is always talking. These are the thinkers and feelers. You can feel the difference in spending time with someone who is present there with you in the moment versus someone who is in their head off with Alice in Wonderland! It just feels different. When I'm with other people, I put my cell phone and my thoughts away. It's incredibly rude to be on your phone in the presence of others and it's also rude to not be paying attention. Living inside your head is a very lonely place. The present moment is where everything exists. Presence is incredibly sexy!

A relationship is not a band-aid for your life or to make you complete. If you feel incomplete, go and get yourself completed before dating. Two incompletes do not make one complete. Going into any relationship with excessive emotional baggage is a death wish. Both of you will work it out on each other! All your insecurities will rear their ugly heads at the most inopportune times! When emotions are high, intelligence is low. And when intelligence is high, emotions are low. Make it a point to always stay calm, especially when something triggering happens to you. This is when you'll need your emotional intelligence the most. Becoming manic solves nothing.

While we all do thrive on and need support of various kinds from family, friends, and loved ones, we should never look to a man to heal or complete us. Imagine walking into a relationship where the guy constantly needs reassurance from you. It's so draining. Would you really want to enter any relationship like that? How well do you think it'll go? I can't even see a capacity for growth in such a situation. A man should come complete with an option to upgrade, meaning, if he can't grow with you, he's got to go. Humans are constantly growing, expanding, and creating new desires. I enjoy being part of a power couple.

You can control your emotions. I promise you. It's normal to feel your feelings. You just don't want to swim in the negative ones, which is what we tend to do. Please start telling yourself that you have complete control over what and how you choose to feel. Knowing you can control your emotions is the first step. The two biggest tools for gaining emotional intelligence for me have been self-awareness and self-reflection. I am very mindful of my emotions, especially when something triggering occurs.

Did you ever watch men about to fight? It's quite interesting to watch. A friend of mine was teaching me a lesson about emotions and showed me the beginning of this boxing match. One guy was jumping around almost bouncing off the walls and threatening to crush the other guy. He was just so flooded with emotion. His opponent stood there, calm as can be. As soon as the match started, the emotional guy went after the calm guy, and he got knocked out in one quick punch! It seemed that the calm man kept his energy to himself, and it came out in the form of victory! Choose to see it however you like, but the bottom line is usually the calmer person gets further. The quiet one is usually the confident one in just about any type of situation. The person who is just reacting, amped up, or overly emotional is likely afraid and seems to fail more times than not. Spend some time getting to know yourself and how you react to different situations and life events. How can you improve? When emotions are high, intelligence is low and when intelligence is high, emotions are low. I repeat it so much because it's very important for you to understand that. When it comes to the initial stages of dating, you want your intelligence to be high and your emotions to be low. This will keep you in control and stop you from making poor dating decisions.

The purpose of our emotions is for guidance. Good feelings guide us to desired things and negative feelings guide us away from undesired things. Your intuition is also a feeling. Intuition helps you in the form of thoughts, nudges, urges, feelings, and sometimes just "knowing." Many times, I just know things I just have no rational way of knowing and it always comes to pass that way. One thing I do know is that my thoughts create my feelings. In a book by RJ Spina, *Change Your Mind*, he says that things begin in this order: desire, intention, thought, feeling, action, and eventually then behaviors. Are your thoughts mostly positive or negative? Are they helpful or hurtful? Do they say, "I can," or "I can't?" Starting now, decide that you will choose your thoughts and feelings from this moment forward. It's not that difficult to do. If you are attracted to a man that you know is unhealthy for you and you can't seem to break away, start asking yourself all the things about him that you don't like. I bet there are many. Focus on those. Forget any perceived good qualities this man may have. Sour milk is still sour milk. Continuously tell yourself all the things you don't like about him. In time, these repeated thoughts will turn into feelings, negative feelings, which will make it that much easier to walk away. Always choose you.

When struggling with an intense or difficult emotion, find your center. I know this is not easy to do in the heat of the moment but do it anyway. Practice patience because patience and peace go hand in hand. I practice patience daily, and I experience peace through meditation. You can go on Google or YouTube to find guided meditation on just about anything you need help with. Although I feel quiet meditation is the most helpful type of meditation and you start by simply observing your thoughts. I know it's hard and I know you think you can't do it, but I know you can do it! In time, you'll begin to hear your guides and receive guidance from them. Talk about a nice perk of attaining peace! And again, feelings should be felt, processed, and released. Unless it's a feeling of joy, please don't swim in it. I've learned how much smarter it is to process and release these feelings. Things that seem unfair to us can trigger angry feelings within us. The best thing you can do for yourself when an emotional situation arises is to just sit with it and feel it out.

My favorite way to ground or to center myself is by doing deep breathing exercises. Breathwork is amazing! Especially if you've had any type of trauma in your life and we all have. I find so much relief in a long exhale. Typical calming breathing involves a regular inhale through the nose and an extended exhale through the mouth. If you're not familiar with somatic breathwork, it releases stored emotions and trauma from the body. Over time this builds up and can create physical illnesses. Self-care is so beneficial to living your best life! You can find so many somatic breathwork practitioners online who do sessions via Zoom. Another wonderful technique to calm your emotions is called "box breathing." Imagine going up the left side of a box while inhaling for a count of ten seconds. Then imagine holding your breath across the top of the box for ten seconds. Next, exhale for ten seconds (or longer) as you envision yourself going down the right side of the box. And lastly, pause for ten seconds on the bottom side of the box. Exhaling for a long time awakens your parasympathetic nervous system which controls your relaxation response, regulates your digestion, your heart rate, and your breathing. I highly recommend doing this whenever you feel anxious or triggered. It's so important that you try to feel calm under all circumstances. You can center yourself by standing barefoot in grass, hugging a tree, or holding a grounding stone such as black kyanite. Grounding keeps you centered and connected to the Earth. It has tons of health benefits too!

Try to be consciously aware of what you're feeling. Self-evaluation and observation are both useful tools in helping to create the life you truly want to live. Because your thoughts create your feelings, you can see why it's so important to try to keep negative thoughts at bay. Negative thoughts become negative emotions. We each think almost 100,000 thoughts each day and while that may seem like a lot, I'd bet many of them are on a loop. Can you control your thoughts? You sure can! I keep it really simple. If I don't want it, I don't think about it. Many of us stay stuck in "lack thinking," which only shows us what we feel is missing from our lives. This kind of thinking is detrimental because it lowers your vibration and will keep you in a cycle of lack. Don't think about what is missing from your life. Instead think about what you are glad that you have and any other amazing things you would like to create. Visualize the future you'd like to experience, again, using all five senses to make it real. Do this as often as possible. Thinking about good things will promote good feelings. We attract things at the level we are feeling at. If you are thinking good thoughts and creating good feelings, you are on the path to manifesting something you desire that feels good!

Of course, being a human being means that sometimes your emotions might get the best of you no matter how hard you might try to control them. Things that we feel strongly about or people that we have deep connections with can bring out the most intense feelings within us. Realize that these are called "triggers," and when a person emotionally triggers you it's because of something unhealed inside of you that light is being shed upon. It's trying to show you something in your shadow that you're likely unaware of. Our shadow is our inner child, or all the suppressed or repressed parts of ourselves that tend to come out at inconvenient times if we haven't done any inner work on ourselves. If you haven't cultivated a deep sense of inner peace that you can return to, this will be very challenging to do. Consistently make the choice to feel better each time you find yourself in any type of emotionally charged situation and you will never again be a slave to your emotions. Do your best to be present and embodied and your emotions have less of a chance of taking you over. You are the conqueror of your body and your mind as RJ Spina likes to say. Meditation can help control your emotions also.

Emotional and mental strength are things that take time to develop. While believing you can do something is important, it's also incredibly important to believe in yourself. Know that you can be strong, even if you never were before. Please don't concern yourself with what other people will think. Believing you can control your emotions and choosing to control them is what you need to do. Happiness is a practiced energetic state that you can create within yourself by practicing feeling good as often as you possibly can. Find all the good in each moment. Having emotional intelligence in your relationship can make or break it! Please use the tools I've provided throughout this chapter on emotional intelligence, as well as the communication tips provided at the end of Chapter 10.

CHAPTER 13
RAISE YOUR STANDARDS

"When you raise your standards, only the boys will disappear.
The men will step up to meet them."
~ Mandy Hale

Do you know what you want in a man? I can hear you thinking about all the things that you know you don't want, but what is it that you DO want? Thinking about what you don't want (contrast) will reveal to you what you do want. Don't hover on the negative. In other words, get clear. For instance, your last three boyfriends were slobs and never cleaned up after themselves. After work, you would spend an hour cleaning up just to be able to sit down in comfort. When you focus on being with the slobs and what you don't want, what are you attracting more of? More slobs! Thinking about slobs will attract more slobs into your life! How can we turn this around? Think about what it would feel like to be with a man who not only picked up after himself, but always did extra around the house. How does that feel to you? Keep feeling that because it's what you want! Envision it too! Now you're more in alignment with your desires than you were when you were focused on the negative. Each time you think of a negative, turn it into a positive. Take what is unwanted to learn what is wanted and focus on what you want! Then visualize with all your senses and keep meditating. Now you're getting somewhere!

Have you taken the time to do the inner work on yourself that we've discussed in prior chapters? Do you feel that you have a pretty good understanding of yourself and your desires? Have you made a conscious choice to "own your value?" You need to do that before you'll meet a quality man. Quality men want quality women. A quality woman is a woman who values herself and is aware of what she needs and wants to be happy. She doesn't compromise her value to accommodate a man either. Does this feel like you? Are you ready to go out into the world and attract an amazing man? Do you feel ready? Most importantly, do you feel strong? It's likely that you will be tested and tested often. You need to feel incredibly strong and have convictions in your new beliefs, faith, and view of men and the world in general because your faith and beliefs will be tested. Whenever you have doubts about what to do in any given situation, ask your gut what to do. See what feels right. Know in advance what you want and be willing to walk away from what you don't want. All the things that you say no to send a very clear message to the Universe about your desires. Settling sends the Universe a message that you will accept less than everything you want. I'm not a fan of settling. What are your standards regarding men now? What kind of man do you want?

Maybe even more importantly than knowing what you want in a man, you need to know who you are, on a very deep level. The situations that we just discussed above will test your resolve. If you have a rock-solid idea of who you are, nobody can make you bend against your will. When you encounter a questionable situation, where you find yourself second-guessing yourself, don't. You're a Goddess. You have infinite power. You contain within you the ability to create worlds. The next time you question your worth, remember you do deserve to have it all! Deservingness is a choice that we each make for ourselves. If you deem yourself to be less than others, you make it so. Choose differently. Choose to know that you're powerful and the only person who can stop you from having it all, is you.

If you begin dating after reading this book and find yourself dating guys similar to guys from your past, take note. Never say yes to something you really want to say no to. If you find a man causing you to compromise your beliefs or values, walk away. Your gut will tell you if he's wrong for you. Only you will know what feels right and which guy is worth seeing again. Hopefully you've done your inner work and won't settle just to not be alone. If he says or does things that feel off to you in some way, don't ignore it. A new guy may likely put on his best face to impress you, and if he screws up with his best, what else is left? Things feel bad for a reason. Usually because they're out of alignment with our truest desires. What do you do if you find yourself attracting low quality men? Raise your standards again and keep raising them. Again, we live in a mirror universe, so you're always attracting to you who you are being. Change who you are on the inside and magnetize a man like you on the outside! Your standards are the basis of what you want in a man. If you've truly done everything outlined in this book and are still repeating unwanted patterns with men, please check out my recommended reading list in the back of this book for further help.

You need to know what you want before you can get it. Figure it out now. Do you want to tolerate another loser who will offer you a house date where you cook, or a classy guy who takes you to dinner and a movie? Would you say yes to Netflix and chill? If you accept the house date, you're saying yes to something you don't want. That's lowering your standards. That's a big no-no. *People will always push you as far as you let them,* and this is not the guy for you, not if you have done the inner work. You stop settling when you know your value. If a guy I don't know or barely know expects me to go out of my way for him, he will soon become a part of my past. A man who is truly interested in you will be going out of his way for you and never the other way around.

If at any point in time you feel too focused on any relationship that you're in, put the focus back on yourself. Read this book again and do the exercises I've discussed. Focusing too much on another person always has a funny way of waking you up to help you shift the focus back to yourself. You can't control or change another person. In your own life, you can move mountains. Always shift the focus back to you. Men fall in love with women who are in love with themselves. Are you in love with yourself? Loving yourself is the beginning of the life you were meant to live. Never having loved yourself truly means never having lived because life starts there. Once you truly love yourself, the right thing to do is to think of one person that you've loved more than anyone. It can be an ex-boyfriend, child, parent, anybody really. And I am talking about unconditional love because there is a huge difference. This person that you loved so much, so unconditionally, you would do just about anything for them, wouldn't you? Now, make this person be **YOU**. Love yourself unconditionally more than anything in this world. That is the greatest gift that you could ever give to this world and to yourself. When we heal ourselves at the individual level, we also heal the world!

There's no reason why you can't have your cake and eat it too! The only one stopping you is you. Do you believe you can have what you want? Notice if you said no, because if you believe you won't, you surely won't. Play God. If you were God and said, "Let it be," it would be, right? Stop questioning yourself and your desires. You can have more than what you want. Please note here that nice is just another word for doormat. Nice or kind people are generally doing things for you so that one day they can cash in, and you will owe them a favor! Be careful of meeting "nice guys," as they generally don't have a backbone and won't offer you the mental challenge or "push back" that all humans crave in relationships. Additionally, being called the "cool girl" isn't so cool either. It means anything goes with you and you won't speak up when you're opposed to something. Notice if someone refers to you as nice, kind, or cool, because they're saying you're a pushover. Guys know they can get away with a lot and you won't say a word about it. Women need to present a mental challenge to capture the heart of a divine man. You need to know what you stand for and what your boundaries are. Don't let men cross your boundaries and don't let anyone think you're too kind or too nice. I'm not suggesting that you're mean or nasty, but rather authentic. Only you know what authentic behavior is for you.

CHAPTER 14
ALWAYS BE WILLING TO WALK AWAY

*"Have the courage to walk away, those that value you will want
you back and those that do not won't hold you back."*
~ Trevor Driggers

It has been said that the only certainty in life is change. I know this is a complete and total contradiction to the concept that, "people don't change," which you and I both know to be untrue. People change all the time, for better or for worse. The famous saying that, "people don't change," is meant in the context of dating someone and waiting on that person to make a change that YOU want them to make in their own lives because it is something that is displeasing to you. People don't change for others, only for themselves. True and lasting change must always come from within because that is the only place you will find true and lasting inspiration. For example, exercising or getting in shape to impress a certain person is external motivation; meaning, it does not come from your soul. It's not something that you desire for yourself. Doing it for yourself will raise your chances of succeeding immensely! Remember, we only fail at something if we quit trying.

Over time, we all change. Some people grow apart, and some people grow together. Surely in your lifetime you have had friends come and go. When we change our vibration, which always begins with how we think and feel, we've changed. We're meant to evolve and grow on this journey we call life. We're meant to learn lessons and be challenged by those lessons. Many times, people may test us. If you're in a relationship with a man who refuses to commit or plays games or takes you for granted, you need to be willing to walk away. One of my favorite YouTubers, Fareen Ash, discusses how she was dating her fiancé for several months and he knew that she was interested in marriage, but he made no attempt (yet) to be exclusive with her. One night he attempted to make plans with her only to discover that she had a date with another man. Imagine his surprise when she told him she had a date with someone else! I'm pretty sure this is when he decided to be exclusive with her and she's a top rated YouTuber discussing relationships. She knew she wanted marriage and a family, and this man had not even asked her to be exclusive yet, so she played it smart and kept her options open. Always keep your options open! Once a man sees that you're attached to him or that you've stopped dating other men without him asking you to be exclusive, he knows he's got you! And once he's got you, he doesn't have to try as hard. Men never value what comes easily to them. Never. Never let them feel so comfortable with you to the point that they know you'll never leave. Never, ever, tell a man that he is "it" for you!

MEN NEVER APPRECIATE WHAT COMES EASILY TO THEM

And what most women don't know is that a truly masculine man enjoys earning his woman's love! Nobody appreciates anything that comes easily to them. The harder we work for things, the more we value them. Just think of trophies, awards, plaques of accomplishment, certifications, and degrees. They're all paper, tin, or wood, but we value them so much from the amount of effort that we put into attaining them! And this is exactly how men feel about women. We need to stop tolerating men who don't continue pursuing us by being romantic and doing things to make us happy. Never get too comfy or let him think for a second you won't leave!

Men, Sex, and Sports

One thing I've learned that sex and sports have in common is the thrill of the chase or the pursuit. Instead of using the word "sex," I am going to use the term, "pursuing a woman." Men love to do things for women to earn their affection. They love the game. Is it clicking for you yet? Sports are a big, popularized metaphor for sex. The chase, the pushing other "players" away, the constantly trying to "score" on the other team, and then finally, getting that ball into that hole, whatever type of hole it may be! And whoever gets the most balls in the most holes the most times is crowned the winner! Men love to watch the game for the chase. It's a game and a chase and they love it! If you hand yourself over easily with no resistance, men will likely vanish from your life in the blink of an eye! The harder a man must work to get you, the more he VALUES you! If a man doesn't value you, the relationship will go nowhere. Men need to be needed. They'd never tell you that openly, but every man wants to be with a woman who makes him feel needed. If a man offers to help with something, always say yes. This doesn't mean you can't also be independent too, but don't let the guy feel useless. Men love feeling useful so always include them in projects or any type of work where you could use the help.

If you're a woman stuck in a dead-end relationship, leave. If you don't feel cherished, safe, loved, and protected, leave! If your man isn't meeting your needs in any way at all, leave now. Many men are in their wounded feminine energy, and they expect a woman to just give to them. This is how masculine women and feminine men go together, like a tornado meeting a volcano. (Thanks Eminem!)

If you don't feel excited to see your man, he's not the right man for you! You should feel some type of inner stirring around the man that you love! If a man isn't romancing you or he's not making any effort, leave. The answer to men who can't treat you how you deserve to be treated is always to leave! My mom used to say that men were like buses and another one will be coming in ten minutes. Don't get attached to a man just because you're lonely either. I know for a fact that great men do exist! If you believe that they don't exist, then that will be your experience. Our beliefs create our experiences by showing us what's possible for us and if we don't believe that something is possible, it's not! You need to get out of your own way here! Never get attached to a man.

We live in a world of mirrors where everyone we know is mirroring to us precisely how we feel about ourselves on the inside. To change what we see in our outside world; we must first change what is happening in our inside world. In other words, we need to change how we think and feel about ourselves at our core level or our identity. If you want to get into this more, checkout the book *Psycho-Cybernetics* by Maxwell Maltz. This book teaches you how to change your entire identity. You really need to know that you're totally amazing! You can't just think it in words though. You need to feel how loved and valuable you are just for being alive. We are all extensions of the creator, which makes us all creators. Self-love is the best kind and really the only kind because any type of love or emotion that we ever feel is always coming from inside of us!

You don't need to be thin, beautiful, or successful to be in a happy and loving relationship. You don't need to look like a supermodel to have a happy marriage or partner. You don't even need to be fully healed, mentally or physically. Feminine energy leans back and receives. If you have problems receiving, it's because you've been in your masculine energy for far too long. Please don't beat yourself up about this, as it wasn't your fault. You did it as a survival mechanism. I know that many of you have also grown up in very difficult childhood dynamics that possibly turned you into people pleasers! We've put ourselves last to put everyone else first. Do you know what happens when we do that? We abandon ourselves. Come back to your body and stay in it. You do that by honoring what you want and what you don't want. We need to learn how to ask for what we want in life, especially if we've never done that before. **Speaking up is very important**. Don't live your life on autopilot or by default. When you don't make choices for yourself, others will make them for you! Having strong boundaries is also another way to respect yourself. Know what you will or won't tolerate.

Never let a man feel like you're not willing to walk away, especially in the beginning stages of the relationship before you have the talk about commitment. Men must know that you're always willing to walk away. This keeps them on their toes and on their best behavior. The fastest way to watch a man stop taking care of himself (and you), is to express to him that you want him and only him. Once a man knows that you're attached, he will attempt to start getting away with small things like being messy, and as time goes on, it'll escalate to bigger things. You always need to take good care of yourself and choose yourself first. A good man will honor this and love you for it even more. There are tons of great men out there who are looking for a woman just like you!

In this mirror universe, everyone you meet is mirroring an aspect of you back to you. Please read that as many times as you like or look up what the universal "Law of Attraction" is. Better yet, read up on the law of assumption. Once we change internally, our outside world must also change. All change starts from within. Before Michelangelo painted the Sistine Chapel, he had an image of it in his head. Before Edison created the light bulb, he had a vision of it inside him. Everything starts on the inside, including your dream relationship. Make sure you're visualizing and fantasizing frequently about your desired relationship. Be sure to enter yourself into the visualizations using all five senses so your subconscious believes it to be real enough to bring it to you. It's not enough to just see it, but you need to be it. Insert yourself into the vision of you as if you were living that life right now. Don't just watch it, be it now!

I hope this information has helped you love and value yourself so much more! Self-compassion and grace have helped me a ton through this process. Give yourself the love that you always wanted. Be there for you. And once you've crafted your life into your own masterpiece, it'll be that much easier for the right guy to bump into you when you least expect it! If you've truly grown and evolved, you will come face to face with the perfectly mirrored version of you, your true soul mate! Best of luck to you. And I truly love you all!

RECOMMENDED READING

Why Men Love Bitches by Sherry Argov
Never Chase Men Again by Bruce Bryans
He's Just Not That into You by Greg Behrendt
Don't Believe Everything You Think by Joseph Nguyen
Letting Go by David Hawkins
Conversations with God by Neale Donald Walsch
Psycho-Cybernetics by Maxwell Maltz
You Can Heal Your Life by Louise Hay
Atomic Habits by James Clear
Change Your Mind by RJ Spina
The Myth of Normal by Gabor Mate
The Secret by Rhonda Byrne
The Power of Imagination by Neville Goddard
Emotional Intelligence by Daniel Goleman

ABOUT THE AUTHOR

Melanie Joy Vertalino is an author, a teacher, and a certified life coach specializing in relationship coaching. She is also a certified law of attraction life coach. Her passion is helping women become their best selves while teaching them to magnetize their dream man and life. She believes that these goals can be fully achieved by transforming themselves from the inside out. Melanie is a psychic and an empath; she understands people on another level, which helps her to understand the behaviors of others better. Melanie's first book, *An Advanced Gratitude Journal,* has helped countless people align with the source by digging deep into gratitude. This journal goes deeper than most gratitude journals. It presents very in-depth topics to show areas of gratitude you may have overlooked. The second book that Melanie is publishing, titled *The Ladies' Playbook: How to Get Your Way with a Man*, will be released in December of 2024. For more information, please see her website at TheLadiesWay.

Melanie's educational background began with a BA in Psychology from Buffalo State College. She then attended Canisius College to attain an MS in Counseling. After several years of teaching, she decided to return to school to get a teaching certificate and an MS in Education. After years of being an educator, Melanie became enamored with the Law of Attraction. She took a one-year course to become certified as a law of attraction life coach. Since childhood, Melanie has been offering relationship counseling and is sought after for it by her friends. She has been learning about men—how they think, feel, and behave—since her teenage years.

After releasing *The Ladies' Playbook: How to Get Your Way with a Man*, Melanie eventually intends to release a workbook consisting of thirty exercises that correspond with the chapters in *The Ladies Playbook*. She believes knowledge is powerful, but even more powerful when there's inspired action behind it. Melanie has extensive dating and coaching experience, which makes her the perfect teacher to learn from. Keep your eye out for more books by this phenomenal author!